BASIC ECONOMICS
STUD

By J___y Wy___

Table of Contents

Introduction

Thanks for purchasing BASIC ECONOMICS FOR STUDENTS AND NON-STUDENTS ALIKE. I believe that you will find it to be a useful resource: whether you are a student who finds the material easy to understand or a student who is having problems understanding one or more topics covered in your economics class; whether you are taking an introductory economics course or an intermediate-level course; whether you are studying economics because you are interested in the subject or because you are required to take the subject; whether you are a student at all or simply somebody who wants to understand economics; whether you are interested in further studies or if you simply want to become better-informed as a citizen, voter, political "junkie", or somebody trying to keep up with current events; whether you are looking for a learning resource in addition to other resources or if you are looking for a primary resource; or if you are an educator who wants an inexpensive resource for your students to use for any of the above reasons.

You can use BASIC ECONOMICS FOR STUDENTS AND NON-STUDENTS ALIKE to learn the concepts involved in economics whether or not you are comfortable with the graphs, math, and statistics that people normally associate with economics. Graphs are not included, but both the graphs and the concepts behind them are explained; only basic math is included, and you can even skim over the math and still come away with an understanding of the concepts; statistics is not included at all.

BASIC ECONOMICS FOR STUDENTS AND NON-STUDENTS ALIKE is an easy way to learn concepts relating to economics and the economy. It is a product of thousands of hours spent online, teaching basic concepts in economics to hundreds of students worldwide over the course of the past several years. From back and forth communications, I have discovered the explanations for the concepts that students find easiest to understand, as well as the areas that most often get misunderstood and under-emphasized.

I have worked with students located throughout the United States and from many different countries, on six different continents; students from many different school systems with different points of emphasis; students with different levels of knowledge, different backgrounds, and different levels of interest in the subject. I have received numerous comments and testimonials regarding the teaching methods that I incorporate in **BASIC ECONOMICS FOR STUDENTS AND NON-STUDENTS ALIKE**.

The subject matter included in **BASIC ECONOMICS FOR STUDENTS AND NON-STUDENTS ALIKE** comes from a compilation of many different textbooks at the introductory and intermediate levels. My goal was to include every subject in economics that normally will be found in an introductory level textbook of economics, microeconomics, or macroeconomics. Since different school systems, different classroom instructors, and different textbooks cover a slightly different combination of topics, **BASIC ECONOMICS FOR STUDENTS AND NON-STUDENTS ALIKE** is a little more comprehensive than most single introductory textbooks of economics. Some of the topics will be found in introductory classes in some schools, but in intermediate-level classes in other schools.

BASIC ECONOMICS FOR STUDENTS AND NON-STUDENTS ALIKE differs from a normal textbook in a couple of ways. First, while I have made sure to cover the topics that appear in most economics textbooks, and have used several actual textbooks as references for this purpose, all of the text is in my own words. The language that I use is based on what my experience with actual students tells me is the best wording for getting students to understand the material. Second, **BASIC ECONOMICS FOR STUDENTS AND NON-STUDENTS ALIKE** leaves out the many graphs that you would find in a normal economics textbook. My method involves teaching students to thoroughly understand the concepts and assumptions behind the graphs, and I have found that this method works better without the graphs. I anticipate that many readers of **BASIC ECONOMICS FOR STUDENTS AND NON-STUDENTS ALIKE** will have other resources that involve graphs, and that students will most likely need to be able to demonstrate a working knowledge of graphs for their classes in economics. However, I also know that a total reliance on teaching methods involving graphs allows many students to get by with some shortcuts - shortcuts that enable them to learn how to draw conclusions from graphs without a thorough understanding of the economic concepts behind the graphs. For example, you might understand that a market price is the price where the demand curve and the supply curve intersect. But if that is the only way that you know how to explain what a market price is, you really don't understand this basic concept of economics.

While **BASIC ECONOMICS FOR STUDENTS AND NON-STUDENTS ALIKE** contains no graphs, it does describe the graphs that are involved in a "normal" textbook of the same material. If your purpose for using this book does not require knowledge of graphs, and if you are in any way uncomfortable with graphs, then you may skim over the descriptions of the graphs; just be sure to follow along with the concepts and conclusions that go along with the graphs.

I have identified the following groups of people as those who can benefit from this teaching method. These groups represent the target audience for **BASIC ECONOMICS FOR STUDENTS AND NON-STUDENTS ALIKE**:

New students, or students of introductory level courses in economics, microeconomics, and macroeconomics, make up the largest group that this book is designed to help. These are the people for whom I originally developed my style of explanations, and this is the group that has benefitted the most in the past from my teaching style.

Advanced students can also benefit from **BASIC ECONOMICS FOR STUDENTS AND NON-STUDENTS ALIKE**. The material is largely from introductory-level textbooks, but the teaching style emphasizes some of the basic concepts that students tend to overlook as they continue their studies. For example, while different levels of efficiency are present in different market structures, the market structure models themselves are defined using specific assumptions that need to be accounted for in order to move from the models to the "real world". It is a fallacy (non sequitur), then, to use the conclusions that can be drawn from the models as given facts for real-world situations.

Would-be students can use this inexpensive resource as a substitute for the substantial investments of time and money that would likely be required for actually taking a course in economics. This group can learn what such a class would be like, what topics and concepts are involved, and the meaning of the terminology used by students of economics, all without actually taking a course. In addition, somebody who is trying to decide whether to study economics in the future but isn't sure what it is all about can use the information in **BASIC ECONOMICS FOR STUDENTS AND NON-STUDENTS ALIKE** as a valuable part of their decision-making process.

Instructors of economics courses can use this book in a number of ways. The information included here is already being used by many schools in third-world and emerging nations that cannot afford more expensive resources. Instructors can refer students who are having problems with one or more concepts to **BASIC ECONOMICS FOR STUDENTS AND NON-STUDENTS ALIKE** as an additional resource or as an alternative explanation for the same concepts. Instructors of students who wish to study the subject outside of the class curriculum can refer **BASIC ECONOMICS FOR STUDENTS AND NON-STUDENTS ALIKE** as a resource.

Voters and everybody else who wants to be better informed on important issues in society can benefit from learning the concepts and the terminology from a textbook point of view instead of relying on political pundits and one-sided rhetoric for their knowledge of economics and the economy.

BASIC ECONOMICS FOR STUDENTS AND NON-STUDENTS ALIKE is divided into chapters covering broad subject areas of economics. While jumping to specific chapters is permissible, you should keep in mind that many of the subjects build upon material from previous chapters. In writing this book, I assume no previous knowledge of economics concepts or the terminology on the part of the reader. People who don't read this in the order presented may find themselves facing concepts and terminology that they have not been introduced to. As an added help, I have included all of the economics terminology, including the definitions as they apply to this book, at the end in a chapter entitled "Dictionary". Feel free to jump to the dictionary at any time.

The study begins on the next page with an introduction to some basic points of economics that I consider to be prerequisite to the study of larger subject areas.

Basics to Get Started

This chapter covers various concepts and terminology that are important in the general study of economics, but are not necessarily associated with any specific topic under a specific chapter heading. The text in this chapter doesn't read like a story line. Instead, it moves from one term or concept to another.

If you are new to the study of economics, a logical place to start would be to ask: What is economics? For the answer to that question, consider these two facts of life: Human wants are unlimited, and resources are finite. This means that not everybody can have everything that they want. This combination of unlimited wants and limited resources is called scarcity. Scarcity, in economics lingo, is not the same thing as shortage. The term shortage is a completely different concept and will be encountered elsewhere in the study of economics. Scarcity is called "the economic problem". How individuals, groups of individuals, and entire societies deal with this economic problem is what economics is all about. So one definition of economics is this:

Economics: the study of how people choose to use their scarce resources in an attempt to satisfy their unlimited wants.

Economics deals with the answers to the what, how, and who questions: WHAT should be produced? HOW should it be produced? WHO should it be distributed to?

As you will figure out, if you haven't done so already, the study of economics involves a certain kind of logic, a unique kind of thinking. This kind of logic is one of the things that are difficult to define, but you will recognize it when you see it. This form of thinking is called "economic thinking", or the "economic approach".

Economic thinking involves the concept that decisions involve benefits and costs, and include unintended consequences. Economists attempt to include all benefits and costs, including the unintended consequences, in the decision making process. This leads to a thoroughness of the thought process not found in all social sciences.

The study of economics involves the study of efficiency. Efficiency means having the maximum benefit at the least cost. In economics, the types of efficiency include productive efficiency, allocative efficiency, and economic efficiency:

Productive efficiency: using the least cost combination of resources to produce a specific output level.

Allocative efficiency: producing what the consumers want at a price equal to marginal cost (you don't need to worry if you don't know what marginal cost is at this time; it will be explained later).

Economic efficiency: a situation in which both productive efficiency and allocative efficiency exist.

Different levels of study in economics require different levels of mathematical knowledge. The purpose of **BASIC ECONOMICS FOR STUDENTS AND NON-STUDENTS ALIKE** is to teach basic economic concepts, not mathematics. With that in mind, an attempt is made to include only a minimal level of math. However, some math is included, because it is impossible to get very far in the study of economics without encountering some math. I am using the following rule for **BASIC ECONOMICS FOR STUDENTS AND NON-STUDENTS ALIKE** when it comes to using math: Some math is included, but nothing beyond linear algebra; most of the equations that you will see here will be similar to A+B=C, or A divided by B = X%. This will cover the basics, and many students are familiar with the use of such math. For those who are not, much can be learned from reading this book: just skip over the math portions that are not understood. Much can be learned in that manner, but more can be learned if the math is also followed. You also don't have to worry about statistics that are commonly associated with the study of economics. Beginning economics courses generally don't require much knowledge of statistics, and **BASIC ECONOMICS FOR STUDENTS AND NON-STUDENTS ALIKE** does not include such studies.

The study of economics, just like any other discipline, has its own terminology. Some of the terms relate to specific concepts, and the meanings will be explained within the chapters that discuss these concepts. Some of the terms will be found throughout the study of economics, across a wide variety of topics. Here is one example:

Firm; business firm; company; enterprise; business; seller; producer

These are all terms that refer to the same thing; the terms are interchangeable. They all refer to an organization that is controlled by one management structure and offers goods or services for sale in the hopes of earning a profit.

Some people are confused by the difference between income and wealth. Income is the amount of money and other assets acquired during a specific time frame. In the framework of the concept of stocks and flows, income is a flow. Wealth is the value of assets owned at a specific point in time. In the framework of stocks and flows, wealth is a stock.

Some of the terms in economics are terms that may have different meanings in different contexts. In order to avoid confusion, I use only the definitions of these terms that relate to the context that they are used in. For convenience, I have added a chapter entitled "Dictionary" which contains the terms used in **BASIC ECONOMICS FOR STUDENTS AND NON-STUDENTS ALIKE** as well as a definition for each term; a definition that is specific to the context used here. The list of terms in the Dictionary chapter is much more complete than a list found in most textbook indexes. If it is a term found in the study of economics, and if it is also a term found within the text of **BASIC ECONOMICS FOR STUDENTS AND NON-STUDENTS ALIKE**, then it is included in the Dictionary. Since I use only context-specific definitions, many of the terms are defined in my own words.

On the subject of economic analysis, the study of economics necessarily involves learning many different topics and concepts. **BASIC ECONOMICS FOR STUDENTS AND NON-STUDENTS ALIKE** is divided into various topics accordingly. In order to fully understand and analyze real life situations, knowledge of many different topics must be understood and incorporated into the analysis. Most topics are taught in terms of specific relationships, with assumptions made in order to isolate these relationships.

These assumptions include one involving "ceteris paribus", or "everything else held constant or equal". This assumption allows for a better understanding of the concepts being studied. It is necessary to make this assumption for studying concepts, but it is an assumption that does not hold true in the real world and must be relaxed when applying these concepts to real-life situation. In the real world, everything else is not constant or equal. The economy is dynamic, and changes are always occurring. With constant changes, real world analysis means that disequilibrium of some kind is always involved with any situation. Knowing which relationships are in equilibrium and which are in disequilibrium for any given situation is a key to proper economic analysis.

Equilibrium is a very important concept that is involved in all areas of economic analysis. I have found that while textbooks and classroom instruction generally explain this equilibrium well as individual economic principles are introduced, the concept of equilibrium is still often under-emphasized. If you keep in mind that it forms the basis for ALL areas of analysis, you should be able to have a clearer understanding of economic analysis. The definition of equilibrium as it relates to the study of economics:

Equilibrium: a situation in which no forces exist to create changes.

This definition can be applied to all areas of life, not just the areas normally associated with the study of economics.

The opposite of equilibrium is disequilibrium. When disequilibrium exists, the current situation is not sustainable in the long run and will change, with changes moving towards a situation of equilibrium.

Since the real world economy is dynamic, composed of many different inter-relationships, the concept of equilibrium is actually more of a process or a direction of movement, rather than a state of being. One fallacy that I see as common among politicians and others discussing the economy and concepts in economics is the fallacy of non sequitur. In this case, non sequitur means using the conclusions that are drawn from the models and theories as if they were real-world facts instead of what they really are: models based on specific assumptions that may not hold true in the real world.

When you hear people, especially politicians, discuss economic issues, you often hear them talk about what should be done, or what course of action should be followed. Such statements are called normative statements. Normative statements are statements about "what ought to be". Other kinds of statements you may hear in relation to economics are called positive statements, which are statements of facts, statements of the results of studies, etc. Positive statements include no value judgments, while normative statements include value judgments. The economic approach requires the avoidance of using normative statements. Only positive statements should be used in applying the principles of economics to real-world situations. The use of normative statements is one trap to avoid when studying economics.

For the economic approach, it might be helpful to note three other common mistakes to avoid:

1. Economics involves the study of human behavior. This should be done by assuming that people's behavior is governed by "rational self-interest" (more on that a little later), instead of assuming that behavior is governed by ignorance. Don't assume that people behave in a certain way because they are "too stupid" to behave rationally. Instead, you should assume a rational reason for behavior.

2. Avoid the fallacy of composition. This is the fallacy of saying that what applies to one will apply to many. For example, one person might be better off by saving more and spending less, but the consequences are different if everybody makes the choice to save at the same time.

3. Just because an association between events can be found does not mean that one event caused the other. Two things happening together could be a coincidence. Or there may be a provable statistical connection between two events. But just because the events can be linked does not in any way imply that one caused the other.

I mentioned the term "rational self-interest". This is the assumption in economics that the choices people make are done rationally, based on the information known at the time, in an attempt to maximize their satisfaction. This satisfaction is known in economics lingo as utility (the term "utility" will come up often in the study of economics). "Rational", in this sense, does not imply that everybody would make the exact same decision when confronted with the same choice, using the same available information. Different people can make different decisions and each can still be rational. Different people have different goals, different attitudes, and different costs.

Some economists use the term "bounded rationality" instead of "rational self-interest" in order to emphasize the fact that people do not have perfect knowledge at the time that they make decisions. But the terms are interchangeable. Also, it is important to note that "self-interest" is not the same thing as "selfish". People who are acting in rational self-interest, and are trying to maximize their satisfaction, can very well do so by helping others, giving to charity, or making numerous sacrifices.

In the study of economics, the term "goods and services" is often encountered. Some comments about terminology would be appropriate at this time. "Goods" refers to physical products, while "services" refers to non-physical products. In terms of what is available for sale, an example of a good is a new car on a car lot. An example of a service is housecleaning. For many types of economic analysis, these terms are used together to indicate that the analysis applies to both together; thus the term "goods and services". Because this is used so often in economics, it is often shortened to "goods". It may seem confusing at first to have this second meaning of "goods", but the context should allow you to know which meaning is being used in each instance.

Some other terminology to be familiar with:

Economic good: Something that wouldn't exist in sufficient quantities if it were free. This covers the vast majority of goods.

Free good: Something that there would be enough of even if it were free. It is very difficult to find a real-world example of a free good. Some people say that air is a free good, but in some locations, "clean air" is not free; there is a cost involved.

Economic bad: Something that people pay to have less of; pollution, for example.

Resources or economic resources: Anything used in the production of other goods and services. These include land, labor, and capital.

Land: This includes such things as minerals, timber, and water, as well as the actual land itself.

Labor: The physical and intellectual services of people. This includes training, education, and peoples' abilities. Entrepreneurship is a special class of labor, but some economists have classified it as a fourth type of resource.

Capital: Manufactured products such as machinery and equipment that are used in production. Capital in this sense is separate from forms of financial backing such as stocks, bonds, etc. Those kinds of assets are known as financial capital, as opposed to physical capital. In terms of factors of production, capital only refers to physical capital.

These different types of resources produce earnings of their own, and these earnings all have their own terminology: land earns rent, labor earns wages, and capital earns interest. If entrepreneurship is listed as a fourth type of resource, then its earnings would be called profit.

The study of economics is generally divided into two broad categories: microeconomics and macroeconomics.

Microeconomics is the study of economics on the individual level: the individual firm, the individual consumer, the individual worker.

Macroeconomics is the study of economics at the level of the economy as a whole, or an entire industry or sector of the economy as a whole. Economic sectors are classified as the consumer, or household sector; the business sector; the government sector; and the international sector.

It is often talked about, and joked about, that economists tend to disagree on just about everything. Since economists, who are supposed to be the experts in the field, cannot agree or come to a consensus, then people, and especially government officials, often suggest that their own instincts and opinions are just as good as anybody else's, including the so-called expert economists. These people often draw erroneous conclusions by making this assumption. The truth is, economists actually agree on almost everything. One thing that economists always agree on is the logic of economics itself, something that often gets excluded by other people, including politicians. The few things open for disagreement are the only things that the public sees regarding economic thought. These points of disagreement are the things that tend to make headlines. Since the public sees only the disagreements, they falsely conclude that the norm is for economists to disagree among themselves.

There are very good reasons behind the disagreements that do exist. Economies are very complex. They involve literally millions of inter-relationships and transactions every day. In order to be able to draw conclusions, economists develop simplified models to explain these relationships one at a time. Earlier I mentioned the term "ceteris paribus", which is Latin for "other things being equal". This means that economists assume that the other millions of relationships are irrelevant to the study at hand. But this assumption only holds true within the economic model, the theory being studied. In the real world other things never remain constant. Isolating specific relationships does yield valuable, statistical correlations that aid in the understanding of how things work. Remember, though, that correlation does not prove cause and effect.

Keeping the assumptions in mind, and having the ability to understand what changes from the theory to the real world when the assumptions are lifted, often separates the "good" economists from the rest.

Economists have used many studies to create many simplified models of the complex world. Sometimes, the complexity is compounded by the fact that the relationships studied take time to develop in the real world. By the time they do, other factors will have changed. The result of all the complexity is that different interpretations of the conclusions that can be drawn from looking at different models will exist. This is one of the causes of disagreements among economists, and has led to different economic "schools of thought". These differences often show up in public as being associated with different political philosophies. It doesn't mean that economists cannot agree on anything, and it doesn't mean that economic study is not worthwhile.

Another criticism of economists is that they are not 100% accurate in their predictions. However, they are not supposed to be 100% accurate. Predicting specific real-world results with complete accuracy is not their jobs, and they shouldn't claim that it is. Their jobs involve studying the models, the evidence that they have at their disposal, comparing the evidence to the current and complex real world situation, and then drawing conclusions based on what they believe is likely to occur based on the information that they have at hand. These are economic forecasts, not quite the same thing as predictions of the future. But the complexity of the real world, compounded by the fact that the results will depend on future decisions that will be made by imperfect humans, means that "results may vary" when it comes to forecasts about the economy.

If you are in an economics class learning microeconomics, you likely will be required to spend a lot of time learning how to graph various items relating to the revenue, costs, and profit of a firm. Since I am including no graphs in **BASIC ECONOMICS FOR STUDENTS AND NON-STUDENTS ALIKE**, I will limit the discussion of these topics to definitions of the various terms and concepts behind these graphs. I am not trying to downplay the importance of these topics; my expectation is that those who will need to spend time on the graphs for their classwork will be using **BASIC ECONOMICS FOR STUDENTS AND NON-STUDENTS ALIKE** as a supplemental resource while the rest of you will be better served by familiarizing yourselves with the terminology. The remainder of this chapter concerns this terminology. I present these terms and their definitions in the form of a list, with no organized discussion. The terms in the list are grouped together by subject. You will find many of these terms discussed in later chapters. You can find all of them listed in the Dictionary at the end of **BASIC ECONOMICS FOR STUDENTS AND NON-STUDENTS ALIKE**. I would suggest that unless your schoolwork gives you a reason to do otherwise, you might be better off just reading through the list so that you have at least a vague idea what is included, and not spend time trying to memorize these terms. You can always use this section or the dictionary as a reference for later in your studies.

The list of terms relating to revenue, costs, and profit starts here and continues to the end of this chapter:

Total Physical Product, TPP, and Total Product are interchangeable terms. They refer to the total number of units of output for a given quantity of a variable input.

TPP at first increases rapidly, then increases slower, eventually will decrease (for example, too many workers will mean that they lose time by bumping into each other or waiting to share resources).

Diminishing Marginal Returns is a concept based on the idea that when units of a variable input are added, output per input will initially increase, but eventually output will decrease with additional units, and ultimately becoming negative. Diminishing marginal returns kicks in at the point where output decreases with additional units of a variable input.

Marginal Physical Product (MPP) at first increases, but then it decreases constantly until turning negative.

Average Physical Product (APP) will be below MPP as MPP increases and above MPP when MPP declines.

MPP will cross APP at the point where APP is maximized.

The relationship between MPP and APP as indicated above means that when marginal is above average, the average increases; and when marginal is below average, the average decreases.

Cost curves are mirror images of product curves.

Total Cost (TC) increases as output increases: at first rapidly, then more slowly, then rapidly again.

ATC is also called SRATC in the short run.

ATC = TC divided by Total Output

The ATC curve is U-shaped.

16

Marginal Cost (MC) equals change in Total Cost divided by change in Total Output; but MC also equals change in Variable Cost divided by change in Total Output, since VC are the only portion of TC that changes with output.

Change in MC at first decreases with more units of output, then steadily increases; this means that MC = ATC when ATC is at the minimum point of its U-shaped curve.

Total Fixed Cost (TFC) is constant at all output levels.

Average Fixed Cost (AFC) decreases as output decreases.

The Average Variable Cost (AVC) curve is U-shaped.

MC = AVC when AVC is at its minimum.

The cost terms listed above all relate to short run situations.

In the long run, all costs are variable because, by definition, all possible short run situations are available for consideration in the long run.

The LRATC curve connects all possible SRATC curves.

The shape of the LRATC curve depends on the sections that correspond to economies of scale and diseconomies of scale. Economies of scale exist when long run unit costs decrease as output increases. Diseconomies of scale exist when long run unit costs increase as output increases.

When economies of scale are present the LRATC curve slopes downward; when diseconomies of scale are present the LRATC curve slopes upward.

The LRATC curve can be any shape, but is typically shown as U-shaped, having a section with economies of scale and a section with diseconomies of scale. This U-shape is not universal but is considered to be the most typical shape.

Minimum Efficient Scale (MES) is the lowest point on the LRATC curve.

Planning Horizon is another name for the long run, since all planning options (nothing fixed) are open.

Profit is the amount remaining from total revenue after all costs have been taken into consideration.

Profit is a flow concept. It involves activity over a period of time rather than balances at a given point in time (which would be a stock, not a flow, concept). The period of time in question is called the accounting period.

In economics, two kinds of profit will be encountered: accounting profit and economic profit.

Accounting profit includes the items that a business will include in its income statement. This includes total revenue and the costs incurred from fixed and variable costs. Since these are costs that the business must actually pay out, they are called explicit costs. Accounting methods that a business uses to match costs and revenue may create a timing difference within any accounting period between actual outlays and fixed costs shown on the income statement. But these costs are paid at some point in time, and are still explicit costs regardless of the accounting method used.

Accounting Profit = TR - TC

TC = TFC + TVC

From the standpoint of economic analysis, Economic Profit often is more important than accounting profit. Economic profit is profit above normal profit, as explained in the following paragraph:

A firm will only remain open for business as long as it can earn enough accounting profit to prevent its investor owners from investing in something else instead. If investors can earn a higher return somewhere else, they will sell their interest in the business and invest in something else instead. At the same time, if a business can earn more money doing something else, it will change its overall business strategy and move into a different market. Since a certain amount of accounting profit is required to keep the business operating in its current form, these profits represent a cost of the business. In the study of economics, they are called normal profits. Because normal profits are necessary for a firm to remain open for business, normal profits are costs of the business. However, they are not explicit costs because they do not represent any actual money that the business has to pay for expenses. They are called implicit costs. Normal profits, or implicit costs, are opportunity costs. They represent the benefit that would be received from investing in the next best alternative to the business. Normal profit is the amount of profit required to prevent resources from being diverted to another use. When these opportunity costs are deducted from accounting profit, the result is called economic profit.

Opportunity Cost = value of the next best option

Economic profit = accounting profit minus opportunity cost

The opportunity cost in this equation may be shown with a different name, such as normal profit, implicit cost, even the cost of equity capital.

Positive economic profits mean that a business (or industry) will be more profitable than alternatives. This will attract new investments, or more competing businesses in the industry.

Negative economic profits mean that a business (or industry) will be less profitable than alternatives. This will result in less money being invested, or businesses exiting the industry.

Zero economic profits represent a situation of equilibrium. This is the level of profits that provides no incentive for investments or businesses to either enter or exit.

In economics, whenever the single-word term "profit" is encountered, its context should determine whether it refers to accounting profit or economic profit. In general, when the context involves such things as demand and supply, and cost and revenue curves, any mention of the word "profit" would refer to economic profit.

Marginal Revenue Product (MRP) is the additional revenue generated by adding one more unit of a variable input, such as labor. This depends on two things: the MPP (see above) and the slope of the demand curve.

MPP is the number of additional units of output generated by an additional unit of a variable input. Selling additional units at a constant market price would mean that MRP equals the price times the change in quantity.

In most types of market structure, however, the market price will not remain constant. For normal goods, the market, or industry, demand curve, as well as the demand curve for an individual firm in most market structures, slopes downward. This means that selling additional units of output will require lowering the price of the output.

Marginal Revenue (MR) is the additional revenue generated from selling one more unit of output. With a downward sloping demand curve, MR is below the market price.

Total revenue is maximized at the point where the demand curve is unit elastic. At the point where total revenue is maximized, marginal revenue is equal to zero, by definition.

At prices higher than the revenue maximizing price, demand is elastic and MR is positive: Increasing output from this section of the demand curve will increase total revenue.

At prices lower than the revenue maximizing price, demand is inelastic, and MR is negative: increasing output from this section of the demand curve will decrease total revenue.

What this means for a downward sloping demand curve: the MR curve slopes downward, lies below the demand curve, is steeper than the demand curve, and crosses the horizontal axis (is equal to zero) at the quantity of output that maximizes total revenue.

In the special cases of a horizontal demand curve (such as for an individual firm in a perfectly competitive market) and a vertical demand curve, the MR curve is equal to the demand curve.

Profit maximization: MR=MC

The formula MR=MC should be forever ingrained into the minds of everybody who has ever studied economics. This is probably the formula most known, most quoted in microeconomics (along with the related formula QD=QS). As a formula, MR=MC is at the heart of every management decision regarding how much to produce and what price to sell it for.

Also, MR=MC as a profit-maximizing point has universal application: it is a mathematical principle that applies to every situation. Whether a firm is in perfect competition, is a monopolist, or lies somewhere in between, the same profit maximizing rule applies.

Simply stated, this formula means that profits are maximized at the level of output where marginal revenue is equal to marginal cost.

The reason why the MR=MC formula for profit maximization always works:

At any output level where MR is greater than MC, the last unit produced added more to total revenue than to total costs, and profits increased. When profits are rising, increasing output will increase profits. At any output level where MR is less than MC, the last unit produced added less to total revenue than to total costs, and profits decreased. When profits are falling, decreasing output will increase profits. Combining the above statements, profits can always be increased by changing the output level if MR>MC or if MR<MC. As long as profits can be increased, they are not maximized. The only production level that will maximize profits, then, is at the only remaining possibility: MR=MC.

Supply and Demand

Why are some items that are for sale relatively inexpensive, and others cost so much that you wouldn't ever think about buying them?

Why does your neighborhood have the types of businesses that it has, and not others? Why do you see shelves in a store empty some of the time, and seemingly overflowing at other times?

Why are some types of businesses forced to compete with many others, while other types of businesses are free to operate with little or no competition?

Why do some businesses thrive while others are shutting down? Why do prices change?

The answers to these and many other common questions are based on supply and demand.

It has been said many times that the study of economics is the same thing as the study of supply and demand. If you understand supply and demand, the saying goes, you already understand economics. Indeed, all topics studied in economics classes are related very closely to supply and demand. And it is true that the study of all other economics topics builds on the concepts of supply and demand.

An understanding of supply and demand is essential to an understanding of everything that is related to the study of economics. If you have difficulty with any topic in economics, it is likely that a more thorough understanding of supply and demand will solve that problem. A lack of a thorough understanding of supply and demand can cause misconceptions later on in your studies and even in other areas of life, including political viewpoints.

In short, this topic is probably the most important topic in the entire study of economics. You will want to understand what is in this chapter before trying to master the other topics in economics.

Basic definitions relating to demand:

Start with the law of demand. The law of demand states:

The quantity of a specific good or service that people are willing and able to purchase decreases as the price increases, and increases as the price decreases, as long as the price is the only thing that changes.

You may see the law of demand defined using slightly different words, but the meaning is the same. Implied in the definition is a specific time frame. The word "quantity" does not have much relevance unless a specific time frame is involved. However, just knowing that a time frame is involved, and not having to know what the specific time frame happens to be, will be sufficient for most kinds of analyses. The time frame remains implied and not repeatedly stated during an analysis.

Also, it is important to note before moving on, the fact that this definition states that price and quantity demanded move in opposite directions: when one increases, the other decreases. This is called a negative correlation.

The law of demand requires an understanding of the definitions of two more terms: demand and quantity demanded.

Demand: The amount of a specific good or service that people are willing and able to purchase at every possible price.

Quantity demanded: The amount of a specific good or service that people are willing and able to purchase at one specific price.

These two definitions (demand, quantity demanded) form a distinction that is very important in the study of economics. This distinction also happens to be one that many students have trouble understanding. For this reason, I have included a more detailed description of this distinction below.

But first, a few more definitions of terms that are relevant to demand, and the distinction between demand and quantity demanded:

Factors of demand: Factors of demand are the price of the good in question, plus other things that determine the level of demand. You will find that an analysis of demand will require the price of the good in question to be considered separately from the other things that determine demand. The other things are called determinants of demand.

Determinants of demand: Consumer income, consumer tastes, the prices of complements, the prices of substitutes (you may find the prices of complements and substitutes lumped together in a category called "the prices of related goods"), consumer expectations, and the number of potential buyers. A more detailed definition of each determinant of demand follows:

Consumer income: The more income that people have, the higher the demand for goods and service in general. This means that for each specific normal good, income and demand are positively correlated: income and quantity demanded change in the same direction. An inferior good is the opposite of a normal good. An inferior good is one that people buy less of if their incomes increase. They choose to use the higher income on more expensive substitutes, and buy fewer of the inferior good. An inferior good is an exception to the law of demand that states that a negative correlation between price and quantity demanded exists.

Consumer tastes: When consumer tastes change, the demand for specific goods and services also changes. Styles come and go, fads come and go.

Prices of complements: Complements are two goods that consumers tend to purchase together. Since consumers purchase two items as if they were one (a package deal), if the price of one of the items changes, so will the price of the package deal, and the demand for the other item will change accordingly. An increase in the price of one good or service leads to a decrease in the demand for its complement; a decrease in the price of one good or service leads to an increase in the demand for its complement (negative correlation).

Prices of substitutes: Substitutes are two goods that, in the eyes of consumers, can be substituted for each other. If they spend their income on one, they won't want to spend their income on the other. They may prefer one to the other, but if the price of one changes, it may influence which one they prefer at the different relative price. An increase in the price of one good or service leads to an increase in the demand for its substitute; a decrease in the price of one good or service leads to a decrease in the demand for its substitute (positive correlation).

Consumer expectations: If consumers believe that prices will change in the future, or their incomes will change in the future, it may affect how much of a specific good or service they purchase now, instead of later.

Number of potential buyers: Since market demand is equal to the sum of all individual demands, the number of potential buyers will influence the total demand for a good or service.

More definitions:

Demand schedule: A list of prices and their corresponding quantities demanded.

Demand curve: A graph of the demand schedule. Often a curve turns out to be a straight line, but in economics it is still referred to as a curve. By tradition, the demand curve is a graph with an origin of (0,0), with quantity on the horizontal (X) axis and price on the vertical (Y) axis. The demand curve slopes downward because of the negative correlation in the law of demand.

Market demand curve: The sum of all individual demand curves in a given market.

Change in demand: When one of the determinants of demand changes, demand changes; the entire demand schedule, or demand curve, changes. This means that the quantities demanded at every price change. This is shown by a shift in the demand curve. If demand increases, the demand curve shifts to the right (or up, depending on what terminology you use). If demand decreases, the demand curve shifts to the left (or down).

Change in the quantity demanded: If the price of the good or service in question (the good or service that is used to plot the demand curve) is the only thing that changes, then demand does not change. The demand curve does not change (or shift), but the price and quantity combination moves to a different point on the existing demand curve.

As stated above, many students have difficulty grasping the distinction between demand and quantity demanded. The first thing to do in trying to understand this is to look at the difference in the definitions of the two terms. Demand refers to every possible price; quantity demanded refers to a specific price. If a price changes, then such a change is already covered by demand; demand includes all prices. So a change in price will not change demand, it will only involve a movement along an existing demand curve. That would be called a change in the quantity demanded. In order for demand to change, there must be a change in a non-price factor of demand (one of the determinants of demand). In that case, the quantity demanded will change at every price, and the demand curve will shift as a result.

Another way to look at it that may be helpful to some students: if the change is plotted on an axis (price is plotted on the vertical axis), then the change is a change in the quantity demanded. If the change is not plotted on an axis (the determinants of demand are not listed on an axis), then the change is a change in demand.

Before we move on to a discussion of supply in the supply and demand model, we have a couple of models designed to explain the law of demand: utility and indifference curves.

The term utility is used often in economics. Utility is a concept used to help explain the choices that consumers make. This helps to explain demand, especially the downward slope of the demand curve.

Utility refers to the amount of satisfaction, or happiness, that individuals receive from the choices that they make. Each person is unique. Different people receive satisfaction for different reasons. They will make different choices even if the circumstances are the same. Because of this, the concept of utility explains how making different choices can still be consistent with the basic assumption in economics that people behave rationally.

Utility (satisfaction) comes from more than just financial wealth and material possessions. Sure, people can derive satisfaction from wealth accumulation. But people also derive satisfaction in other ways. People may be satisfied knowing that they are helping others. Such charity takes many forms, and involves many choices as well. People may gain satisfaction from accumulating many friends, or maybe just having a few very close friends. Some people gain more satisfaction from leisure than others. Many people enjoy hobbies, and different people are willing to devote different amounts of their time and incomes to an unlimited number of potential hobbies. Some people prefer current consumption while others prefer future financial security.

All of these considerations, and more, contribute to different rational choices being made by different people.

Since utility comes from the choices that people make, a cost is always involved. If there were no costs, then people wouldn't have to make choices. But when someone decides what to do with a specific time frame or a specific sum of money, they have to give up using that time frame or that specific sum of money for a different activity.

The cost of a choice is more than just the amount of money or time that has to be spent on that choice. The cost of a choice is the amount of satisfaction (utility) that has to be given up because another choice was not made instead.

This means that the true cost of any choice is its opportunity cost. Since choices often involve more than two options, and only one of the options can be chosen, the opportunity cost is a measure of the utility of the best alternative to any given choice. It would not make sense to add up utilities for several options when only one of them can be chosen.

This concept of measuring opportunity cost brings up another concept in economics: the concept that utility can somehow be measured. It is true that people everywhere do not go around all the time computing a number in order to make the best choice every time that a choice is made. But people do make choices because of the way they envision the benefits and costs involved. Without even realizing that they are doing so, people are making measurements regarding utility. Whichever options are available, people choose the one in which the perceived benefits most outweigh the perceived costs.

Another concept in economics involving utility and choice is that choices do not occur in a vacuum. Every choice relates to choices that have been made previously. Suppose, for example, that you have a favorite song that you haven't heard in a long time. Now, suddenly, it has been made available to you so that you can listen to it as often as you like. Since you haven't heard it for a long time, you might make it a priority to listen to it immediately. All other options that you have for using this time frame will have to wait. So you listen to it once, and it makes you very happy (you receive a high utility value from this). You want to hear it again. You listen to it a second time immediately after the first time, and the utility is still high. But not quite as high as the first time, because you had to wait so long to hear it the first time. In fact, every time that you listen to it consecutively, the utility is going to be somewhat less than the previous time.

This is the concept of diminishing marginal utility. Each time the same option is chosen within a specified time frame, the utility will be less than the previous time. Somewhere along the line, with diminishing marginal utility, the utility received from making the same choice over again will be less than the utility that could be received from something else, even if that "something else" initially had a lower utility value. You will receive more utility if you choose to "spend" your next choice on something else instead.

As the same choice continues to be made, with less utility received each time, eventually you could end up actually decreasing your total utility: the last choice gave you a negative amount of utility. Maybe you eat so much that you get sick. When marginal utility becomes negative, this is called disutility.

When making choices, the available options might be complicated somewhat because different choices might involve a different (explicit) cost outlay. One option might take up more of your time than another option. One option might require you to spend more of your income than another option.

For example, suppose you decide to go out to dinner with friends. You will enjoy going out, enjoying the company of your friends, so you will be happy (have positive utility) with whatever restaurant choice is made. You could go to a fast food restaurant and be happy. You would be even happier (have a higher amount of total utility) going to a fancy restaurant, but it would cost more. If you spent more for dinner at a fancy restaurant, you would have less money left over for other things. So, which option would be better, fast food or fancy restaurant?

The answer is that you would choose whichever one gives you the most utility per unit of cost. The value you place on a fast food meal, divided by its cost, can be compared to the value you place on dining in a fancy restaurant, divided by its cost. You would choose the one that gives you the highest value (utility) per unit of cost.

This concept, maximizing marginal utility per unit of cost, applies as well to a series of choices. Each choice depends in part on previous choices. Each subsequent time that the same choice is made will provide less total utility than the previous time that particular choice was made (diminishing marginal utility). But presumably, the cost will be the same. Additional units of the same choice will provide you with a lower benefit at same cost. Therefore, the marginal utility per unit of cost will change over a series of choices.

In order to maximize total utility from a given budget, the budget will be spent over a series of choices, each one based on maximizing utility per cost, and each choice giving less utility per cost than the previous time that choice was made, until the income is spent with the marginal utility per cost for each option being equal.

This situation, where all income is spent and the marginal utility per cost for each option is equal, is called consumer equilibrium, or the Equimarginal Principle. Consumer equilibrium can be shown mathematically as:

$$MU(A)/P(A) = MU(B)/P(B) = ...MU(X)/P(X)$$

Where A = one option, B = another option, and X represents each additional option to be considered.

The concept of utility leads us to the reasons behind a downward sloping demand curve. Each individual consumer will allocate income among the various consumer choices in such a way that the ratio MU/P for each consumer good will be equal.

If the price of one good increases relative to other goods, then the ratio MU/P will decrease, and the consumer will purchase this good in a smaller quantity. If the price of one good decreases relative to other goods, then the ration MU/P will increase, and the consumer will purchase this good in a higher quantity. For each individual consumer and each individual good, more will be purchased as the price decreases. This means that an individual's demand curve for each good is downward sloping. Notice that this involves price changes relative to the prices of other goods.

The market demand curve is simply the sum of all individual demand curves. With decreasing marginal utility and consumer equilibrium, the result is a downward sloping demand curve.

Consumer surplus measures the difference between the amount that a consumer is willing to pay for a given quantity of a good, based on its marginal utility, and the amount that the consumer actually has to pay for that quantity, based on the market price for that good. Since marginal utility decreases with each additional unit purchased, a consumer will require a lower price in order to consume a larger quantity.

We move now from a look at utility to a look at indifference curves, but we are still dealing with demand.

Indifference curve analysis is a simplified, graphical economic model that helps to explain consumer choice. This model assumes that an individual consumer is making a choice between two goods, and will choose to purchase an optimum combination of the two goods within a given budget.

It must be assumed that for a consumer, more of a good is always preferable to less.

An indifference curve plots all combinations of the quantities of two goods for which a consumer has no preference of one combination over others. If the quantity of one good is increased, then the quantity of the other good must be decreased. Otherwise, the consumer would not be indifferent. More is better.

An indifference curve is bowed inward toward the origin. This is because of decreasing marginal utility. As more of one good is consumed, the amount of total utility added will decrease. Since adding one additional good means decreasing the other good, the consumer would only be indifferent between two bundles if they lie on a curve that is bowed in.

An indifference map can show a series of many different indifference curves together. An indifference curve that is further from the origin would be preferable to one that is closer to the origin.

Indifference curves cannot intersect each other. If they did, they would violate the assumption that more is better.

The optimal bundle of the two goods for the consumer would depend on the amount that the consumer has budgeted for the combination of the two goods.

Given a fixed price for each good, the consumer can spend the entire budget on one good, all of the budget on the other good, or any combination of the two goods which spends the entire budget. A budget line (or budget constraint) would be a downward sloping straight line on an indifference map, representing all combinations of the two goods that add up to the total budget for the two goods.

Since utilizing an indifference curve that lies as far from the origin as possible is preferred, the optimal bundle would be the one that lies on the budget line and touches the right-most indifference curve. Given the bowed in shape of indifference curves, this would be only one point on the indifference map.

We now move from demand to supply in our analysis. The wording of the discussion of supply is very similar to the wording of the discussion above relating to demand.

The law of supply states:

The quantity of a specific good or service that producers are willing and able to offer for sale increases as the price increases, and decreases as the price decreases, as long as the price is the only thing that changes.

You may see the law of supply defined using slightly different words, but the meaning is the same. Implied in the definition is a specific time frame. The word "quantity" does not have much relevance unless a specific time frame is involved. However, just knowing that a time frame is involved and not having to know what the specific time frame happens to be will be sufficient for most kinds of analyses. The time frame remains implied and not repeatedly stated during an analysis. Also, it is important to note before moving on, the fact that this definition states that price and quantity supplied move in the same direction: when one increases, the other also increases. When one decreases, the other also decreases. This is called a positive correlation.

The law of supply requires an understanding of the definitions of two more terms: supply and quantity supplied:

Supply: The amount of a specific good or service that producers are willing and able to offer for sale at every possible price.

Quantity supplied: The amount of a specific good or service that producers are willing and able to offer for sale at one specific price.

These two definitions (supply, quantity supplied) form a distinction that is very important in the study of economics. This distinction also happens to be one that many students have trouble understanding. For this reason, I have included a more detailed description of this distinction below.

But first, a few more definitions of terms that are relevant to supply:

Factors of supply: Factors of supply are the price of the good in question, plus other things that determine the level of supply. You will find that an analysis of supply will require the price to be considered separately from the other things that determine supply. The other things are called determinants of supply.

Determinants of supply: The prices of resources, technology and productivity, expectations of producers, the number of suppliers, and the prices of alternative goods and services that the firm can produce. A more detailed definition of each determinant of supply follows:

Prices of resources: The prices of resources, or inputs, are a cost of production. If production costs increase, producers will offer a lower quantity of goods and services for sale at every price; if production costs decrease, producers will offer a higher quantity of goods and services for sale at every price. A negative correlation exists between the prices of resources and the quantity supplied. This is because higher costs will lower the profits available at each price. When costs increase, firms will be able to cover their costs and earn an acceptable profit only by lowering their output, all else equal.

Technology and productivity: If resources are used more efficiently, the costs of production decrease.

Expectations of producers: If producers expect a future change in any of the determinants of supply, it may cause them to change the current supply in order to lock in profits.

Number of suppliers: If more firms produce a good or service, the supply of that good or service will increase.

Prices of alternative goods and services that the firm could produce: If the opportunity cost of a firm changes, it would change the profitability of a given quantity of a specific good or service that the firm supplies.

More definitions:

Supply Schedule: A list of potential prices and their corresponding quantities offered for sale.

Supply curve: A graph of the supply schedule. Often a curve turns out to be a straight line, but in economics it is still referred to as a curve. By tradition, the supply curve is a graph with an origin of (0,0), quantity on the horizontal (X) axis, and price on the vertical (Y) axis. The supply curve slopes upward because of the positive correlation in the law of supply. Suppliers will by willing to offer a higher quantity for sale only if they can receive a higher price in order to cover increasing costs.

Market supply curve: The sum of all individual producers' supply curves.

Change in supply: When one of the determinants of supply changes, then supply changes. The entire supply schedule or supply curve, changes. This means that the quantities supplied at every price change. This is shown by a shift in the supply curve. If supply increases, then the supply curve shifts right (or down, depending on what terminology you use). If supply decreases, the supply curve shifts left (or up).

Change in the quantity supplied: If the price of the good or service in question (the good or service that is used to plot the demand curve) is the only thing that changes, then supply does not change. The supply curve does not change, but the price and quantity combination moves to a different point on the existing supply curve.

As stated above, many students have difficulty grasping the distinction between supply and quantity supplied. The first thing to do in trying to understand this is to look at the difference in the definitions of the two terms. Supply refers to every possible price; quantity supplied refers to a specific price. If the price changes, that change is already covered by supply; supply includes all prices. So a change in price will not change supply, and it will not shift the supply curve. It will only involve a movement along an existing supply curve. That would be called a change in the quantity supplied.

In order for supply to change, and for the supply curve to shift, there must be a change in a non-price factor of supply (one of the determinants of supply). In that case, the quantity supplied will change at every price, and the supply curve will shift as a result.

We now put what we just learned about demand and about supply together, and move to a discussion of equilibrium in the supply and demand model.

The demand curve shows the quantity of a good or service that buyers are willing and able to purchase at each price. It slopes downward, indicating an inverse (negative) relationship between price and quantity demanded.

The supply curve shows the quantity of a good or service that producers are willing and able to offer for sale at each price. It slopes upward, indicating a positive relationship between price and quantity supplied.

The demand curve and the supply curve will intersect at only one point, where the quantity demanded is equal to the quantity supplied. This intersection point is called equilibrium. It represents the price and quantity that exchanges will take place in a free market.

Equilibrium is a point where no forces exist that will cause any changes in the market. Once the equilibrium point is reached, the market will stay at that point unless something else changes. For supply and demand, such a change would be a change in a determinant of supply or a determinant of demand, causing the supply curve or the demand curve to shift.

At any price other than the equilibrium price, the quantity supplied and the quantity demanded are not equal. If the price is above the equilibrium price, the quantity supplied is greater than the quantity demanded, and the difference is called a surplus. If the price is below the equilibrium price, the quantity demanded is greater than the quantity supplied, and the difference is called a shortage.

The surplus and shortage situations can be seen as resulting from the fact that the supply curve slopes upward while the demand curve slopes downward. If the price rises above the price where the quantity supplied is equal to the quantity demanded, purchasers would want to purchase a lower quantity while suppliers would want to supply a higher quantity. If the price falls below the price where the quantity supplied is equal to the quantity demanded, purchasers would want to purchase a higher quantity while suppliers would want to supply a lower quantity. The law of supply and the law of demand make this true.

Surpluses and shortages represent situations of disequilibrium. Disequilibrium is not sustainable as long as the price is free to adjust. Market forces will move the situation back to an equilibrium condition.

If a surplus exists, suppliers will have an increase in unsold inventory. The suppliers will lower their prices and reduce the quantity being made available for sale in order to reduce the unsold inventory. Lower prices and decreased production will be more profitable than unsold inventory.

If a shortage exists, producers will see that inventories are depleted and consumer demand is not being met. Suppliers will see this unmet demand as a source of potential profits. The suppliers will raise their prices and increase the quantity being made available for sale in order to take advantage of consumer demand.

Many people make the mistake of equating the concept of shortage with the concept of scarcity. Actually, in economics, these terms are unrelated. A shortage is a situation in which the quantity demanded is greater than the quantity supplied. Scarcity refers to the fact that human wants are infinite while resources are limited (more would be wanted at a price of zero than would be available).

In equilibrium, the price and quantity exchanged in a free market will not change unless one of the determinants of supply or demand changes. But what would be the result of such a change? The equilibrium price and quantity can change only if demand or supply changes. In turn, demand or supply changes only when there is a change in one of the determinants of demand or supply.

First, we will look at what happens to equilibrium whenever a change in demand occurs. Remember that the determinants of demand are consumer income, consumer tastes, the prices of complements, the prices of substitutes, consumer expectations, and the number of potential buyers. When one of the determinants of demand changes demand also changes.

When demand decreases, it means that consumers are willing and able to purchase a lower quantity at each and every price. Looking at it another way, it means that it will take a lower price to induce consumers to purchase the same quantity. For any given supply, a decrease in demand means that the market price will decrease while the quantity sold will also decrease. This is represented on a demand and supply graph as: the demand curve shifts left (down); this new demand curve intersects the given supply curve at a point where the new equilibrium shows a lower price and a lower quantity than the old equilibrium.

When demand increases, it means that consumers are willing and able to purchase a higher quantity at each and every price. Looking at it another way, it means that consumers will pay a higher price for the same quantity. For any given supply, an increase in demand means that the market price will increase and the quantity sold will also increase. This is represented on a demand and supply graph as: the demand curve shifts right (up); this new demand curve intersects the given supply curve at a point where the new equilibrium shows a higher price and a higher quantity than the old equilibrium.

We now look at what happens whenever a change in supply occurs. Remember that the determinants of supply are the prices of resources, technology and productivity, expectations of producers, the number of suppliers, and the prices of alternative goods and services that the firm could produce. When one of the determinants of supply changes supply also changes.

When supply decreases, it means that suppliers are willing and able to supply a lower quantity at each and every possible price. Looking at it another way, it will take a higher price to induce producers to supply the same quantity. For any given demand, a decrease in supply means that the market price will increase while the quantity sold will decrease. This is represented on a demand and supply graph as: the supply curve shifts left (up); this new supply curve intersects the given demand curve at a point where the new equilibrium shows a higher price and a lower quantity than the old equilibrium.

When supply increases, it means that suppliers are willing and able to supply a higher quantity at each and every possible price. Looking at it another way, suppliers will accept a lower price to supply the same quantity. For any given demand, an increase in supply means that the market price will decrease while the quantity sold will increase. This is represented on a demand and supply graph as: the supply curve shifts right (down); this new supply curve intersects the given demand curve at a point where the new equilibrium shows a lower price and a higher quantity than the old equilibrium.

In summary (nature of change: resulting change in equilibrium price and quantity):

Decrease in demand: decrease in price; decrease in quantity

Increase in demand: increase in price; increase in quantity

Decrease in supply: increase in price; decrease in quantity

Increase in supply: decrease in price; increase in quantity

Often in economics class you will have exercises where you have to determine the effects on the equilibrium price and quantity when both the demand and supply change at the same time. To solve these types of problems, you need to consider the cumulative effect of the multiple changes. For either price or quantity, if all changes are in the same direction, then the cumulative effect will be in that direction. But if changes go in opposite directions, the net effect of the changes will depend on which change is larger. Since these exercises generally don't tell you which change is larger, the answer you are supposed to give is that the net effect is unknown, or indeterminate.

In summary (direction of demand and supply change: resulting change in equilibrium price and quantity):

Decrease in demand and decrease in supply: indeterminate change in price; decrease in quantity

Decrease in demand and increase in supply: decrease in price; indeterminate change in quantity

Increase in demand and decrease in supply: increase in price; indeterminate change in quantity

Increase in demand and increase in supply: indeterminate change in price; increase in quantity

The points made above about equilibrium and changes in equilibrium are based on a simplified version of the real world, which is accomplished by isolating the factors under discussion. Economists use simplified models to study interrelationships. In general, they consider the relationship between two variables at a time; they consider the effects of a change in one of the variables on the other variable. In order to do this in the simplified model, they make the assumption of ceteris paribus. In other words, they assume that everything else remains constant so that they can focus on the specific relationship at hand. In the real world, however, everything else does not remain constant. Changes occur all the time in a dynamic economy. This means that equilibrium is seldom reached, although forces are always at work to move towards equilibrium. The models remain useful, and the studies are valid.

What happens to the equilibrium price and quantity when price controls are present? Price controls are limits set by the government on allowable prices for specific goods or services. An upper limit is called a price ceiling. A lower limit is called a price floor. If a price control prevents the equilibrium price from being reached, it is an effective price control.

An effective price ceiling would be an upper price limit that is below equilibrium. At a price below equilibrium, consumers would demand a higher quantity than producers would supply; a shortage would result. The quantity demanded would be above the equilibrium quantity; the quantity supplied would be below the equilibrium quantity. The amount of the shortage would be the difference between the quantity demanded and the quantity supplied at the price ceiling level.

An effective price floor would be a lower price limit that is above equilibrium. At a price above equilibrium, consumers would demand a lower quantity than producers would supply; a surplus would result. The quantity demanded would be below the equilibrium quantity; the quantity supplied would be above the equilibrium quantity. The amount of the surplus would be the difference between the quantity supplied and the quantity demanded at the price floor level.

Notice that with an effective price ceiling, the quantity supplied would be below the equilibrium quantity. The quantity supplied would be the quantity that is actually exchanged. Consumers cannot purchase what suppliers do not offer for sale. With an effective price floor, the quantity demanded would be below the equilibrium quantity. The quantity demanded would be the quantity that is actually exchanged. Producers cannot sell what consumers will not buy.

This means that price ceilings and price floors both lower the quantity exchanged in the marketplace.

Just as a market exists for final goods and services, a market also exists for the factors of production.

The factors of production are labor, capital, and land. These factors of production must be hired in order to produce the final goods and services. These factors have their own markets and their own supply and demand curves.

The demand for the factors of production is a derived demand. The demand for the factors will be based on the demand for the final goods and services that they are hired to produce. The supply of the factors of production will be based on the opportunity costs for their use. The prices for the factors of production are known by the names of their earnings. The price for labor is the wage rate. The price for capital is the interest rate. The price for land is rent.

Using labor as an example, the demand for labor would be the quantity of labor hours that producers wish to hire, and would be derived from the demand for the goods and services being produced. The supply of labor would be the number of potential workers who would be willing to work at each potential wage rate. In the factor markets, just as in the market for final goods and services, the demand curve slopes downward and the supply curve slopes upward.

Opportunity Cost

Opportunity costs are a part of every decision that people make. In the study of economics, a choice means selecting one alternative or option over all other alternatives or options after weighing the benefits and costs of each option. The option with the highest valued net benefit is the best choice.

When a choice is made, that means that all alternative options have to be given up. These are the forgone options. Since options are forgone, a trade-off is involved.

The opportunity cost of a choice is the value of the next best option that could have been made. It should be emphasized that this definition says "value of the next best option", not "the sum of the values of all options". This is because "all other options together" is not a choice. Only one choice out of the options can be made.

Life involves a continuous series of choices. Each choice is not made in a vacuum, but rather becomes an additional choice to all other choices that preceded it. When a choice is being weighed, the benefits and costs that add to the total of all choices are considered. This means that decisions are made "at the margin". Only marginal changes, which are called marginal benefits and marginal costs, need to be considered. This concept hopefully will become clearer, and will prove to be useful in the study of economics, as the concept of opportunity costs is better understood.

Economists have developed a simplified model to illustrate and study this concept. The model is called the Production Possibilities Curve, or PPC. In real life economies, people can choose between literally millions of different possible combinations of goods, but the PPC model is simplified so that only two goods are considered at a time. The reason for using a simplified model is that people cannot visualize or draw in the many dimensions that a complex economy would require. This simplified model is sufficient to illustrate the concepts involved. Also, the two goods that are considered can be aggregates, such as "defense spending" and "non-defense spending", in order to make the model a little more realistic.

The PPC is a graph that shows the various combinations of two goods that a society can produce given the current level of available resources. Any point on the curve represents a combination that is considered efficient in the sense that it utilizes all available resources. There is no way to move away from any point on the curve to another without giving up something.

Any point inside the curve is considered inefficient because not all available resources are being used: more could be produced without giving up anything. Any point outside the curve represents a production combination that is impossible to produce given the current level of resources.

The PPC illustrates opportunity costs because it shows the trade-offs that are involved. On the PPC, the only way to produce more of one good is to produce less of the other. Such a change in the combination of the two goods would be shown as a movement from one point on the curve to another point on the curve. The amount of one good that is given up to produce more of the other good is the opportunity cost.

The PPC is not normally shown as a straight line, but rather as a bowed-out (convex) curve. This is due to the concept of increasing opportunity costs. "Increasing opportunity costs" is the concept that as more and more resources are diverted from one activity to the other, the marginal cost of the change in the combination that is produced becomes increasingly higher. This is due to specialization. Not all resources used for an activity are going to be equally specialized. As resources are diverted from one activity, the least specialized (efficient) resources would be taken away first. As more and more resources are taken away, however, the marginal resources diverted are ones that are more and more specialized.

It was noted earlier that points outside the PPC are impossible to reach, given the current state of resources. The only way to produce at such a level would be to increase the level of resources. When that happens, the PPC will shift outward. If the additional resources can be used to produce only one good, then the intercept for only that good changes, and the slope of the curve changes (changing the opportunity cost between the two goods).

The level of resources can be increased in two ways: more resources (quantity) can be found or created, or a better way to utilize the resources (technological advances) can be found.

When individuals or countries specialize in the things that they are good at, meaning that they are most efficient at or that have the lowest opportunity costs, then they can trade with others and end up with more than they would have if they tried to do everything themselves.

Specialization and trade are based on the concept of comparative advantage. When one person or country has a lower opportunity cost in a specific activity than another person or country, then it is said to have a comparative advantage in that activity. A comparative advantage indicates an area where specialization should occur in order to increase total production. Then, the good that is specialized in can be traded for the other good.

Even if one party can do more of everything than the other party, both can still gain from specialization and trade due to comparative advantage.

The concept of comparative advantage is often confused with the concept of absolute advantage. Absolute advantage is when one person or country can do more of a particular activity than the other party, based on the total amount of production that is possible for that activity. Absolute advantage has nothing to do with opportunity costs and has no effect on potential gains that can be made from specialization and trade. When determining specialization, only comparative advantage matters.

One type of question that comes up very often on tests relating to opportunity costs, specialization, and trade involves a hypothetical situation of two countries (or individuals) that can each produce two goods in ratios that are given by numbers of units of each good that it can produce. People often ask me questions about this, so I will try to explain it here. I will use two different methods for explanation: a formula and an example. Those who are more comfortable with learning concepts using a formula can start with the next section before proceeding to the example. Those who are uncomfortable with using formulas can just skip to the example.

Using a formula:

This type of question typically looks like this:

Country A can produce (a) number of units of good 1, or it can produce (b) number of units of good 2; country B can produce (c) number of units of good 1, or it can produce (d) number of units of good 2. Which good should each country specialize in?

The answer, using a formula, involves figuring the opportunity cost of each good for each country. The country with the lower opportunity cost for a good should specialize in that good. The opportunity cost for each good can be calculated with a formula:

For country A, the opportunity cost of good 1 is (b) divided by (a). The opportunity cost of good 2 is (a) divided by (b).

For country B, the opportunity cost of good 1 is (d) divided by (c). The opportunity cost of good 2 is (c) divided by (d).

Using an example instead of just a formula:

Japan can produce 5 cars or 10 computers in an hour. The United States can produce 3 cars or 12 computers in an hour. Which good should each country specialize in?

To get the answer, first determine the opportunity cost of the two goods for each country. The country with the lower opportunity cost for a good should specialize in that good, and trade with the other country for the other good.

For Japan, the opportunity cost of 1 car is 2 computers You get this number by dividing the number of computers that Japan can produce (10) by the number of cars that it can produce (5) in the same amount of time. Using the same method, the opportunity cost to Japan for computers is 1/2 (5 divided by 10).

For the United States, you use the same method to calculate the opportunity costs. For cars, that would be 4 (12 divided by 3); for computers, that would be 1/4 (3 divided by 12).

This means that for cars, Japan's opportunity cost is 2 while the United States' opportunity cost is 4. Since Japan's opportunity cost is lower than the United States' (2<4), then Japan should specialize in the production of cars.

For computers, Japan's opportunity cost is 1/2 while the United States' opportunity cost is 1/4. Since the United States' opportunity cost is lower than Japan's (1/4<1/2), then the United States should specialize in the production of computers.

Then, with specialization, Japan can trade cars to the United States for computers, and both countries will have more than if they both produced both products and consumed only what they produced themselves.

To illustrate how specialization can increase total production, start with the above example. Assume that without trade, each country will spend an equal amount of time on the production of each good. That means that in the same period of time, Japan can produce 5 cars and 10 computers, while the United States can produce 3 cars and 12 computers. Together, the two countries produce 8 cars and 22 computers. But with specialization, Japan will produce 10 cars and zero computers, while the United States produces zero cars and 24 computers. Together, with specialization, they end up producing 10 cars and 24 computers. This is an increase of two cars and two computers due to each country specializing in the good that it is more efficient at producing.

You might ask: if they trade, what would be a fair price? The opportunity cost represents the cost of each good for each country if they do not trade. In order to gain from trade, the trade ratio (relative price) should be somewhere between the opportunity costs for each country. Otherwise, one country will not gain from the trade, and the trade will not occur. Since in the above example, the opportunity cost per computer for a car is 2 in Japan while it is 4 in the United States. Any price between 2 cars per computer and 4 cars per computer will benefit both countries.

In this example, you might also be asked which country has an absolute advantage in each good. Since Japan can produce 5 cars in an hour while the United States can only produce 3 cars in an hour, Japan has an absolute advantage in cars (5>3). Since the United States can produce 12 computers in an hour while Japan can only produce 10 computers in an hour, the United States has an absolute advantage in computers (12>10). Absolute advantage is not part of the specialization and trade calculations because it is irrelevant. It would be entirely possible for one country to have an absolute advantage in both goods and still gain from trade, due to different opportunity costs.

It would not be possible for one country to have a comparative advantage in both goods, since comparative advantage is determined by the relative costs of the two goods: if good A costs more in terms of good B, then it follows that good B could not cost more in terms of good A.

Elasticity

Elasticity is a term used in economics to denote responsiveness. It is a measurement of the responsiveness, or sensitivity, of one variable to a change in another variable.

Elasticity has a variety of uses in economics. For example, when a company is deciding on a pricing strategy, it needs to know which proposed price will generate the most total revenue. The elasticity measurement will answer that question. Another example would be a producers' tax proposed on the sale of a particular product. How much of the tax will the producers pay, and how much of it will the consumers end up paying through higher prices? How much tax will be collected? How much will this change the quantity of the product that consumers purchase? The answers depend on the elasticity measurement. In the extreme case of price controls imposed by the government: price controls distort market equilibrium, but how much will output fall with price controls? Elasticity again determines the answer.

Many students have trouble understanding elasticity because the concept is often taught with the use of formulas that look cumbersome and are difficult to memorize. The way I explain it here is different. I teach the concepts behind the formulas. All it takes is an understanding of the concepts, and the formulas just fall into place. There is no need for memorization. Those who understand the concepts, beginning with the explanation in the following paragraphs, should have no difficulty with the numbers or formulas involved.

So here is the first and most important concept. The discussions relating to specific types of elasticity follow from an understanding of this: All types of elasticity are numbers, which represent measurements based on two variables. These measurements are formed using division, and are based on percentage changes in each variable used. These measurements are formed by dividing the percentage change in one (dependent) variable by the percentage change in another (independent) variable. This should be easier to understand by realizing that it is a formula that will yield a number; by putting the dependent variable on top the result will be a measure of its responsiveness to changes in the independent variable.

The key to understanding elasticity is to compare the result of the formula used with the number one (that is the case, mathematically, when division is used to compare two numbers). Higher than one means, mathematically, that the top number is larger than the bottom number; lower than one means that the bottom number is larger than the top number; and equal to one means that the two numbers are identical.

Higher than one (representing a change in the top number that is greater than the change in the bottom number) is relatively responsive, and is called elastic; lower than one (representing a change in the bottom number that is greater than the change in the top number) is relatively unresponsive and is called inelastic; equal to one means that the changes are neutral, and is called unit elastic.

This covers all situations, but the extreme cases where one variable does not change at all with any change in the other variable (either the top or the bottom of the formula equals zero) have special names: Perfectly elastic (zero for the bottom number, or infinite elasticity) and perfectly inelastic (zero for the top number, or zero elasticity).

The price elasticity of demand is probably the first, and most common, type of elasticity encountered in an economics class.

The price elasticity of demand is a measure of responsiveness, or sensitivity, of demand to a change in price. If a business decides to raise the price of a product, it will probably sell a lower quantity of that product, since for a normal good the demand curve is downward-sloping. Or if it decides to lower the price, it will probably sell a higher quantity of that product.

The relative change in the quantity sold, compared to the change in price, is the elasticity of demand. The price elasticity of demand is measured by taking the percentage change in quantity and dividing by the percentage change in price. It is shown mathematically by the formula:

P.E.D. = %change in quantity / %change in price

This formula will always yield a negative number for a normal good. This is due to the law of demand. For a normal good, the price and quantity demanded will always move in opposite directions, due to a downward-sloping demand curve. If it does not yield a negative number, then it is not a normal good but an inferior good. Often, a normal good is assumed for purposes of economic analysis, and it will be shown as the absolute value (the number without the negative sign). This assumption is based on the fact that the negative sign is irrelevant to the analysis. The relationship is still negative, but the negative sign is assumed to be there and is not shown. There are exceptions, for example with a demand equation, when the negative sign is important to the analysis.

For the remainder of this section, in order to keep from repeating this relationship over and over, assume that P.E.D. (or the price elasticity of demand), refers to the absolute value; forget about the negative sign involved, unless it becomes relevant to the discussion.

You don't really have to worry about memorizing this formula, but it helps to be able to recognize it when you see it. You do need to remember that the price elasticity of demand is a measurement of the relative change in quantity to a given change in price, and that by using division to measure this comparison, a higher number for a result will mean more responsiveness, or more sensitivity, of quantity to a price change.

In summary: the more responsive, or sensitive, the quantity sold is to a price change, the higher the price elasticity of demand.

Using division as a method of measurement highlights another important concept. If the quantity changes by the same percentage as the price change, then the answer will have a value of one. If the quantity changes more than the price, the answer will have a value greater than one. If the quantity changes less than the price change, the answer will have a value less than one. This distinction is important because for most types of analysis, the P.E.D., relative to 1, is more important than the actual number itself. In other words, the difference between a price elasticity of 3.5 and a price elasticity of 1.5 is not as important as the fact that each number is greater than 1. This importance will be illustrated in the discussion below about the effect of price elasticity of demand on total revenue.

The price elasticity of demand measurement (absolute value), as compared to one, calls for some terminology that you need to know:

If P.E.D. = 1, it is called unit elastic
If P.E.D. > 1, it is called elastic
If P.E.D. < 1, it is called inelastic

In other words, a unit elastic demand is when the quantity changes by the same percentage as the price change. An elastic demand is when the quantity changes by a larger percentage than the price change. An inelastic demand is when the quantity changes by a smaller percentage than the price change.

You may encounter the extreme cases where either the price change or the quantity change is equal to zero. If there is no price change for any given range of quantities (the formula yields an answer that divides the quantity change by zero, which is defined mathematically as infinity), then it is called perfectly elastic. If there is no quantity change for any given range of prices (the formula yields an answer that divides zero by some number, which is defined mathematically as zero), then it is called perfectly inelastic.

At this time, an example should be helpful.

Suppose that a company sells a product for $2, and at this price the quantity sold is 100 units. If the company raised the price to $3 it could sell 75 units. What is the price elasticity of demand?

To arrive at the answer, start with the change in quantity. The quantity sold will go from 100 units to 75 units, a decrease of 25 units (100 - 75 = 25). This would be a change, from the beginning units sold of 100, of 25/100, or 25%.

Now, figure the change in price, using the same method. The price increased from $2 to $3, an increase of $1. This would be a change, from the beginning price of $2, of $1/$2, or 50%.

Now that you have the percentages, simply divide the quantity percentage by the price percentage, you get 25/50 = 0.5. Always show this number as a fraction. If rounding is necessary, the answers could vary, and the course instructor may set the rules for rounding.

In this example, the absolute value of the result, 0.5, is less than 1. So using the terminology defined above, this would be an inelastic demand. The quantity changed by a lower percentage than the price changed.

Perhaps another example, showing a result with elastic, as opposed to inelastic, demand would be helpful. Suppose you had a situation similar to the example above, where the original (beginning) price is $2, and the original (beginning) quantity sold is 100 units. But now, suppose that in increase in the price from $2 to $3 means that the quantity sold changes from 100 to 25. Using the exact same method to calculate the price elasticity of demand, you get:

The quantity sold will go from 100 units to 25 units, a decrease of 75 units (100 - 25 = 75); a change, from the beginning units sold of 100, of 75/100, or 75%. The price change is exactly the same as in the example above, so that percentage change is still 50%. To get the price elasticity of demand, you divide the percentage change in quantity by the percentage change in price, or in this case 75/50, or 1.5. The price elasticity of demand in this case is greater than 1, since 1.5 > 1. Using the terminology defined above, this would be an elastic demand. The quantity changed by a higher percentage than the price changed.

Determinants of the price elasticity of demand are the availability of substitutes, the degree of necessity, the share of the budget, and the time frame involved.

The importance of the price elasticity of demand for a business can be shown by the effect that it has on total revenue. The business will want to know whether a proposed price change will increase or decrease total revenue.

Total revenue, by definition, is equal to the price times the quantity sold (TR=PxQ). Sometimes, when dealing with elasticity, the language used may call this "total expenditures" instead of "total revenue", but it has the same meaning.

Note what happens to the results of this formula (TR=PxQ) if a price change is involved. Due to the law of demand, the price will move in one direction, and the quantity sold will move in the other direction. Unless the price change and quantity change are both for the same percentage (unit elastic), then total revenue will also change whenever a price change is involved. The question is, does total revenue increase, or decrease? The answer depends on the direction of the price change along with the price elasticity of demand.

If the price elasticity of demand is elastic (greater than one), then that means that the quantity change is more than the price change. So total revenue (price times quantity) will decrease for a price increase, and increase for a price decrease.

If the price elasticity of demand is inelastic (less than one) then the change in quantity is less than the change in price. So total revenue (P times Q), increases for a price increase, and decreases for a price decrease.

In summary:

For an elastic demand a price increase will mean that total revenue decreases.

For an elastic demand a price decrease will mean that total revenue increases.

For an inelastic demand a price increase will mean that total revenue increases.

For an inelastic demand a price decrease will mean that total revenue decreases.

For a unit elastic demand total revenue does not change due to a price change.

You can see from this that the price elasticity of demand is an important element in the pricing decisions of businesses.

One more thing about the relationship between the price elasticity of demand and total revenue: As long as demand is elastic or inelastic, total revenue can always be increased with a price change in the proper direction. The only point where total revenue is maximized is the point where the price elasticity of demand is unit elastic.

The standard method for computing the price elasticity of demand has one major drawback. It is based on the assumption that the company is starting from a position of a specific price and quantity sold, and is considering a change in price. But what about the case where the company is not really "starting" from one particular point? In other words, it does not care whether one price is considered to be the beginning price and the other is considered to be the ending price; it just wants to compare the difference in total revenue resulting from two possible prices.

The drawback in the standard method for calculating the price elasticity of demand is that you often get two different answers depending on which price you designate as the beginning price, and which price you designate as the ending price. In the first example used for that analysis, recall that the prices being considered were:

$2, with sales of 100 units; and $3, with sales of 75 units

The example used $2 as the beginning price, and arrived at a price elasticity of demand of 0.5.

But suppose that $3, with the exact same sales of 75 units, was used as the beginning price, and $2, with the exact same sales of 100 units, was used as the ending price. This is the same situation, using the same numbers, but looking at them from the opposite direction. In this case, the price elasticity of demand would be calculated as follows:

The percentage change in quantity would be 25/75, or 33%. The percentage change in price would be 1/3, or 33%. The price elasticity of demand would be 33/33, or 1.

Going from $2 to $3 gives an answer of 0.5, but going from $3 to $2 gives an answer of 1. Two different methods yield two different answers using the same numbers. Neither method is better than the other as long as specifying a beginning price is not relevant to the situation. To correct for this discrepancy, the midpoint formula is considered to be a superior method.

In economics class, the textbook or the instructor might define the midpoint formula as something like this:

P.E.D. = [(Q2 - Q1) / ((Q1 + Q2) / 2)] / [(P2 - P1) / ((P1 + P2) / 2)]

That formula might look fairly intimidating and difficult to memorize. But luckily, you do not have to actually memorize this formula in order to know how to do the calculations. You only need to understand the concepts behind it, and the calculations will be easy.

If you are trying to memorize this formula, you might not notice that it does not change the concept of the price elasticity of demand. Once you understand that the concept does not change, the calculations become easier without memorization. Refer back to the beginning of this chapter and the first and most important concept of elasticity listed: elasticity (in this case, the price elasticity of demand) is always going to be the percentage change in quantity divided by the percentage change in price. The midpoint formula does not change that concept. The midpoint formula only changes the method of arriving at these percentages. The only new thing that you need to know is the concept behind the different method of arriving at the percentages, and you know how to use the midpoint formula.

For the midpoint formula, instead of dividing the change in quantity by the beginning quantity, and the change in price by the beginning price, simply divide the change in quantity by the average of the two quantities, and the change in price by the average of the two prices. Using the average avoids having to designate a beginning and an ending.

In the example above, the change in quantity is 25; the average of the two quantities is 87.5 ((100+75)/2). The percentage change in quantity, then, using the midpoint formula, is 25 / 87.5, or 28.57%.

The change in price is $1; the average of the two prices is $2.50 (($2 + $3) / 2). The percentage change in price, then, using the midpoint formula, is 1 / 2.5, or 40%.

The price elasticity of demand, using the midpoint formula, is 28.57 / 40, or 0.71 (your course instructor may have you use a different method for rounding).

Recall that the standard method yielded an answer of 0.5 for a price increase and 1.0 for a price decrease, two different answers using the same numbers. The midpoint formula, which is considered superior, yields only one answer, 0.71.

Common types of elasticity, in addition to the price elasticity of demand discussed above, are the price elasticity of supply, the income elasticity of demand, and the cross price elasticity of demand.

The elasticity of supply, also called the price elasticity of supply, is a measurement of the responsiveness of the quantity supplied to a change in price. The formula for the price elasticity of supply is:

Price elasticity of supply = the percentage change in quantity supplied divided by the percentage change in price

This formula will yield a positive number, since the quantity supplied changes in the same direction as a change in price (due to the law of supply, and an upward sloping supply curve).

The numerical value of the price elasticity of supply depends on the ability of suppliers to readily change production inputs. In the short run, some input levels will be fixed. In the long run, all inputs are variable. Time is the predominant factor in determining the price elasticity of supply. The longer the time frame, the more elastic the supply is.

Income elasticity of demand measures the responsiveness of the quantity demanded to a change in income. The formula for the income elasticity of demand is:

Income elasticity of demand = the percentage change in the quantity demanded divided by the percentage change in income

A normal good would have an income elasticity of demand that is greater than zero (a positive number). An inferior good would have an income elasticity of demand that is less than zero (a negative number).

For normal goods, a necessity would have a relatively low income elasticity of demand while a luxury would have a relatively high income elasticity of demand.

The cross elasticity of demand, also called the cross-price elasticity of demand, measures the degree to which different goods are related. It measures the responsiveness of quantity demanded of one good to a price change of another good.

The formula for the cross elasticity of demand is:

Cross elasticity of demand = the percentage change in the quantity demanded of one good divided by the percentage change in the price of another good

A positive number resulting from this formula means that a positive correlation exists between the two goods: the goods are substitutes. The higher the cross elasticity, the closer the goods serve as substitutes.

A negative number resulting from this formula means that a negative correlation exists between the two goods: the goods are complements. Consumers tend to buy the two goods together, as if they were a "package deal".

The concept of elasticity can be used to answer the question "do businesses or consumers pay for a tax on the sale of a good?"

The combination of the price elasticity of demand and the price elasticity of supply will determine how much the consumer and how much the firm pays for a given tax increase.

A tax on the sale of goods (sales tax, excise tax) will ultimately be paid by either the consumer or the firm, or both to some degree, based on elasticity, regardless of who the government actually levies the tax on. If the consumer ultimately pays the tax, it means that the tax incidence falls on the consumer. If the firm ultimately pays the tax, it means that the tax incidence ultimately falls on the firm.

The less elastic the demand and more elastic the supply, the more the tax incidence falls on the consumer. The more elastic the demand and the less elastic the supply the more the tax incidence falls on the firm.

This is because with an inelastic demand, consumers will tend to spend more money with a tax increase. The decrease in the quantity purchased will be less than the increase in the tax. But with an elastic demand, consumers will purchase a smaller quantity with a tax increase, leaving firms to pay for the tax increase with lower revenue.

To the extent that consumers pay the tax, business costs and revenues will not be affected. To the extent that businesses pay the tax, the tax represents a cost of production, and supply will be decreased.

Market Structures

We know that all firms will maximize profits at the output level where MR=MC. In the real world, firms operate in a large variety of environments. These different environments, based on different market conditions, influence the behavior of different firms in different ways.

In order to analyze this real life behavior, economists have identified similarities and differences among firms based on certain characteristics. This has led to the study of firms based on four categories of market structure: perfect competition, monopolistic competition, oligopoly, and monopoly. The characteristics of each market structure relate to differences in the demand curves faced by firms in each category.

The identifying characteristics for each type of market structure include the number of firms in the industry, whether the products are identical (homogeneous), ease of entry for new firms in the industry, and the power that the firm has to influence the price of its products.

Perfect competition and monopoly are extremes at the opposite ends of the competitive spectrum. Most real world firms have characteristics that more closely resemble the monopolistic competition and oligopoly models.

Perfect competition is the market structure that maximizes efficiency, as determined by total surplus. Perfect competition gives consumers more total output at a lower price than other market structures. Firms produce where P=MR=MC, which is at minimum average cost. Advertising is non-existent in perfect competition since products are identical in the minds of consumers. The only competition is price competition, yet each firm is a price taker. Ease of entry and exit means that all firms will earn normal, not economic, profits in the long run.

In monopolistic competition, differentiated products allow for more consumer choices than in perfect competition. Higher prices and lower total output result in less efficiency than perfect competition. Firms do not produce at minimum average total cost.

However, this lower efficiency results from consumer preference for more choices, not from economic profits. In the long run, economic profits do not exist. Advertising is an important part of product differentiation in monopolistic competition.

More than one model is needed to explain the behavior of firms in an oligopoly market structure. Non-price competition can be fiercer than any other market structure; on the other hand, anti-competitive cooperation may exist. Advertising is an important part of competition. So is research and development. Oligopoly is the market structure most responsible for technological advances. Price is above MC, and long run economic profits are possible as long as entry is restricted.

For monopoly, with only one firm in the market, consumers are not given a choice of products. A monopolist has market power, and will set its output at the quantity where MR=MC. This is a lower quantity than the quantity under perfect competition, where MR=demand. At the same time, a monopolist will set its price where the MR=MC quantity equals demand, which is a higher price than perfect competition, where P=MC. With monopoly, advertising and innovation are unnecessary. Long run economic profits are possible.

We will now take a closer look at each of these market structures.

Perfect Competition:

Perfect competition is a market structure in which many firms sell identical products, and no barriers to entry into the market exist for new potential sellers. The characteristics of perfect competition are:

Many sellers: each seller represents a very small portion of the overall market. Since supply and demand in the overall market set the equilibrium price and quantity, one small firm cannot influence the market price. Each firm must accept whatever market price exists. Because of this, firms in perfect competition are called price takers.

Identical products: you may see this referred to as standardized products, or homogeneous products. Consumers have no preference for a product from one firm over the product of any other firm. The products of each firm are perfect substitutes for one another. There is no difference in quality. Consumers would always choose to purchase the product from the lowest priced source. Firms cannot differentiate products in any way, including packaging or advertising.

Easy entry and exit: new firms can enter the market freely. This implies that economies of scale do not exist. Existing firms can just as easily stop production and exit the market.

Perfect information: buyers know where the product is being sold, and at what price. Sellers know the strategies used by their competitors, including price and quantity decisions.

Perfect competition is considered to be the most efficient market structure within any given equilibrium situation. Other market structures have some long term advantages over perfect competition, such as: economies of scale, consumer choices, and incentives for advances in technology. Within any given equilibrium, perfect competition is the most efficient market structure.

In a market (as opposed to an individual firm) supply and demand diagram, the intersection of the supply and demand curves will set the equilibrium price and quantity. In perfect competition, with each firm being a price taker, firms cannot stray from this equilibrium price. The individual firm will produce a quantity so that the sum of all firms will produce the quantity that equals market equilibrium. The least cost component of efficiency will be a product of this market equilibrium. The maximum benefit component of efficiency can be seen from the market supply and demand diagram. Benefit in this context refers to the concept of surplus.

Consumer surplus refers to the difference between what consumers are willing to pay and the amount that they actually pay. The amount that they are willing to pay is based on the demand curve. The amount that they actually pay is based on the market equilibrium price. On a supply and demand diagram, consumer surplus is measured by the area that lies both below the demand curve and above the market price.

Producer surplus refers to the difference between the price the sellers are willing to sell the product for and the price that the sellers actually receive. The amount that they are willing to sell for is based on the supply curve. The amount that they actually receive is based on the market equilibrium price. On a supply and demand diagram, producer surplus is measured by the area both above the supply curve and below the market price.

Total surplus is the sum of consumer surplus and producer surplus. Efficiency is achieved by maximizing total surplus.

On the market supply and demand diagram, the only area that can potentially be a part of total surplus is the area defined by the triangle formed by these three points: market equilibrium, the point where the demand curve intersects the price axis, and the point where the supply curve intersects the price axis. Perfect competition is the only market structure that includes this entire area in total surplus. This makes perfect competition the most efficient market structure.

In economics class, perhaps the most noticeable distinguishing characteristic of an individual firm in perfect competition is the shape of the demand curve it faces. The demand curve is a horizontal line set at the market price. Even though the market demand curve is downward sloping, each individual firm is too small to influence the market price. Since the firm is a price taker, and must accept the market price instead of setting its own price, the demand curve is set at the market price.

The individual firm will set its quantity of output at the level that will maximize profits at the given market price.

Why is the individual firm in perfect competition a price taker? Refer back to the characteristics of perfect competition as a market structure: many sellers, identical products, ease of entry, and perfect information. If an individual firm tries to sell at a price higher than the given market price, it would lose its customers. Given these characteristics, the customers would buy from the sellers who are selling at the lower market price. The firm that sets a price that is above the market price will sell nothing.

An individual firm also would not set a price that is below the market price. The individual firm can set its quantity at an output level that maximizes profit. It can sell all that it wants at the market price. It would have no reason to sell the same quantity at a lower price. Besides, a lower price would mean that the profit maximizing output level would be lower, not higher. This is because of the shape of the marginal cost curve.

In any market structure, profit is maximized at the output level where marginal revenue (MR) is equal to marginal cost (MC). The relevant portion of the marginal cost curve is the upward-sloping portion above average variable cost. In perfect competition, the marginal revenue curve is identical to the horizontal demand curve. This is because a price taker will accept the same price regardless of the level of output.

In perfect competition, then, price equals marginal revenue. Since profits are maximized when marginal revenue is equal to marginal cost, the profit maximizing equation for a perfectly competitive firm becomes:

P=MR=MC

Perfect competition is the only market structure where this equation holds true. You may see it being called marginal cost pricing.

The shutdown rule:

Why is the relevant portion of the marginal cost curve above average variable cost (AVC) instead of average total cost (ATC)? After all, if a firm doesn't cover total costs, it suffers a loss. The answer is that fixed costs cannot be avoided in the short run, and they do not exist in the long run. In the long run, average variable cost equals average total cost, and the firm will produce only if it can cover all costs.

But in the short run, with the existence of fixed costs, average variable cost will be below average total cost. If the market price (same as marginal revenue) is between AVC and ATC, the firm

Monopoly

- Monopoly is a market structure in which one firm supplies the entire market

The product supplies has no close substitutes.

- Because there is only one firm in the market, the firm's demand curve is the same as the market demand curve. Unlike a firm in perfect competition, a monopolist is a price maker. It decides the price at which to sell its product. It also decides what quantity to offer for sell sale. A monopolist has market power.

- Like any firm in any market structure, profits are maximized at the quantity of output where marginal revenue (MR) is equal to marginal cost (MC)

- Since the monopolist sets the quantity where MR=MC, supply is dett determined by marginal cost.

- A monopolist doesn't really have a supply curve. It has a supply point. this is because only one point in a graph factors in price, quantity, demand, and marginal revenue.

- Since other firms are not able to enter the market to take advantage of profit potential, it is possible for a monopolist to earn economic profits in the long run.

- These barriers to enter can be divided into three general classes: natural barriers, anti-competitive behavior, and government-created monopolies.

- Because a monopolist sells a lower quantity at a higher price, all else equal, than a firm in perfect competition, the monopoly market structure is considered to be ~~ineffective~~. inefficient.

Oligopoly

- In economic theory, the oligopoly market structure basically covers cases that do not fit well with the perfect competition, monopolistic competition, or monopoly models.

- Oligopoly covers many different types of situations, and economists have not developed one model that adequately explains behavior for all businesses in oligopoly. However, the oligopoly market structure itself covers more real world situations than the models for the other market structures.

- The characteristics that distinguish oligopoly from other market structures are:
  * few firms. * some if not all are relatively large compared to the overall market sizes;
  * and difficult, but impossible, enter into the market.

- The products may be differentiated or identical.

will suffer more losses by shutting down than it would if it continued to produce. This is because fixed costs do not vary with the level of output. They have to be paid whether the firm produces or not.

Fixed costs become irrelevant to the decision of whether to shut down or not. For example, suppose the market price is $1.00, the current output level is 1,000, fixed costs are $500, and variable costs are $0.75 per unit.

At this output level, total revenue is $1,000. Variable costs are 1,000 x $0.75, or $750. With fixed costs at $500, total cost is $1,250. The firm is losing $250 by producing this level of output ($1,000 minus $1,250). If it shut down, it would still have to pay the entire fixed cost of $500, but it would receive no revenue. It would lose $500 by shutting down. Producing and losing $250 is preferable to shutting down and losing $500.

This is the shutdown rule: a competitive firm should shut down in the short run if it cannot find an output level that will allow it to cover total variable costs. Otherwise, it should continue to produce.

This makes the minimum point of the AVC curve the shutdown price. The breakeven price is the minimum point of the ATC curve. The supply curve for a competitive firm, then, is the portion of the marginal cost curve that lies above the average variable cost curve.

Long run equilibrium in perfect competition is reached when no economic profits exist. Economic profits equal zero. To understand this, remember that equilibrium is a situation in which no incentives for change exist. Also remember that normal profits represent an opportunity cost. Normal profits are required in order to keep a firm from choosing a different option than the current one.

If economic profits (profits above normal profits) exist, then the market becomes more profitable than other markets or opportunities. With ease of entry as a condition of perfect competition, this will be an incentive for new firms to enter the industry. If economic losses (profits less than normal profits) exist, then the market becomes less profitable than other markets or opportunities. With ease of exit, this becomes an incentive for existing firms to exit the industry. Only when economic profits are equal to zero will no incentives for change exist, allowing equilibrium to occur.

With ease of entry and exit a characteristic of perfect competition, economic profits will cause new firms to enter the market. The market supply curve will shift to the right, indicating an increase in supply. This will create a new market price that is lower than the previous market price. The lower market price will eliminate the economic profits, and equilibrium can be reached.

Economic losses will cause existing firms to exit the market. The market supply curve will shift to the left, indicating a decrease in supply. This will create a new market price that is higher than the previous market price. The higher market price will eliminate economic losses, and equilibrium can be reached.

Monopolistic Competition:

Monopolistic competition is a market structure in which entry into the market is easy, and the market has many sellers. These factors make monopolistic competition similar to perfect competition. But monopolistic competition differs from perfect competition because firms in monopolistic competition sell differentiated products.

Consumers consider the products of firms in a monopolistically competitive industry to be close substitutes for one another, but not identical. This is what the term "differentiated" refers to.
Firms in monopolistic competition are free to set their own prices. However, they must do so with the knowledge that at higher prices, some consumers will switch to a competitor's product. The firm that raises its prices will sell a lower quantity.

Because the firm will sell a lower quantity at a higher price, the firm's demand curve is downward sloping. Its marginal revenue curve lies below its demand curve. A profit maximizing firm will sell the quantity where marginal revenue (MR) is equal to marginal cost (MC), but this will be lower than the quantity for a firm in perfect competition.

At the output quantity where MR=MC, the firm can sell at the price where this quantity intersects the demand curve. This price will be higher than the price that equates to MR and MC at that quantity, making monopolistic competition less efficient than perfect competition. This lower quantity, higher price combination is due to the fact that the demand curve is downward sloping. The marginal revenue curve lies below the demand curve. This makes a firm in monopolistic competition similar to a monopoly firm, with the associated loss of consumer surplus and total surplus.

One difference between a firm in monopolistic competition and a firm in monopoly is ease of entry. In monopoly, entry is prohibitive and firms can earn economic profits in the long run. In monopolistic competition, entry is easy and any economic profits will be a signal for new firms to enter the market. In the long run, firms will enter and exit the industry until economic profits are equal to zero.

Because the products of firms in monopolistic competition are close substitutes, but are not identical, firms engage in non-price competition. In fact, non-price competition is often an important part of the decisions made by firms in monopolistic competition. Advertising is important, as firms try to inform consumers of the benefits of their specific products. Brand name recognition helps to build consumer confidence in a particular product, increasing its demand.

Firms can use convenience as a form of non-price competition. Store location can be a convenience to specific consumers. So can the availability of online shopping. The availability of other products and services offered by the seller can also be a form of non-price competition that utilizes convenience for consumers.

Grocery stores often distinguish themselves from the competition by the overall product selection available in their stores, as well as the addition of other products and services at the same location. For example, a grocery store may try to lure in customers by providing a full-service bakery, deli, pharmacy, dry cleaning business, check cashing, video rentals, other product rentals (such as carpet cleaners), delivery services (such as being a drop-off and pick-up location for package delivery companies), wire services such as Western Union, an onsite gas station, recycling services, even banking services.

Other forms of non-price competition include such things as customer service, different product features, style, warranties, and even packaging. Non-price competition is often designed to separate consumers into different groups with separate demands.

Because of the existence of many close substitutes, the demand for products in monopolistic competition is highly elastic. Non-price competition is designed to decrease the price elasticity of demand by rotating the demand curve.

Before moving on to a discussion of the oligopoly market structure, I want to add an anecdote regarding product differentiation. A professor in one of my college courses brought up this question: "What is a better deal for consumers, the brand name products or the less expensive store or generic brands?" He then gave this advice to the class:

Consumers should give the cheaper brands a try, and compare the quality and price of the brand name vs. the store brand or generic brand. Then, consumers will know which they prefer, on a product by product basis, rather than having a strategy of always choosing one or the other. This means maximizing utility per dollar for each type of product. Take canned vegetables, for example. The same consumer may find that more value can be achieved by buying the store brands for canned corn and green beans, while at the same time more value can be achieved by buying the name brand for peas and spinach. This approach means that the value of coupons is lowered, since coupons usually apply only to brand name products. Any savings from using coupons can potentially be offset by savings from using store brands.

Oligopoly:

In economic theory, the oligopoly market structure basically covers cases that do not fit well with the perfect competition, monopolistic competition, or monopoly models.

Oligopoly covers many different types of situations, and economists have not developed one model that adequately explains behavior for all businesses in oligopoly. However, the oligopoly market structure itself covers more real world situations than the models for the other market structures.

The characteristics that distinguish oligopoly from other market structures are: few firms, some if not all are relatively large compared to the overall market size; and difficult, but not impossible, entry into the market. The products may be differentiated or identical.

Firms in oligopoly have a large degree of control over the prices of their products, but at the same time the firms are highly interdependent. Since each firm has a large market share, the actions of each firm are dependent on the actions of competitors. If a firm does not react properly to a competitor's actions, it could lose market share, and profits.

The behavior of firms in oligopoly can be described as either competitive or cooperative. Competitive behavior includes much more than just price competition. Most real world innovation and technological advances come from firms in oligopoly. Firms are continually trying to stay ahead of their competitors with improvements that consumers will want. Firms in oligopoly often spend large sums of money on research and development. Large advertising budgets are also typical in the oligopoly market structure.

No single economic model exists to explain all behavior in oligopoly. Two models that are used to explain competitive behavior are the kinked demand curve and prisoner's dilemma. Also, some behavior by firms in oligopoly can be described as cooperative rather than competitive.

The kinked demand curve model:

Firms in oligopoly face a downward sloping demand curve. If they lower their price, the quantity demanded increases; and if they raise their price, the quantity demanded decreases. Because the demand curve is downward sloping, firms will have to lower the price on all units sold in order to sell more units. This means that the marginal revenue (MR) curve lies below the demand curve.

If one firm decides to lower its price, other firms in the market are likely to match the lower price in order to prevent a loss of market share. The result would be that the firms' market shares will stay roughly the same. The lower prices may induce some new customers into the market, but firms will not be able to "steal" customers away from their competitors if all firms match the lower price. In this situation, the demand curve is inelastic.

If one firm decides to raise its price, the other firms in the market are not as likely to react with similarly raised prices. With a downward sloping demand curve, firms that do not raise their prices will see a chance to gain market share at the expense of the firm that raises its price. Some customers will choose the lower priced substitutes of the firms that choose not to raise prices. In this situation, the firm that raises its price will lose customers to the competition. The demand curve is highly elastic for the firm that raises its price.

In effect, two demand curves exist: one that is inelastic and one that is highly elastic. Each demand curve has only one relevant segment. The inelastic segment is only relevant when the price decreases below the current price. The elastic segment is only relevant when the price increases above the current price. The effective demand curve would be the combination of these two relevant segments. It would be a curve that is relatively flat at prices above the current price, and relatively steep at prices below the current price. A kink forms at the current price.

The price at the kink in the demand curve would have been determined by the demand at the profit maximizing quantity. The profit maximizing quantity is always determined by the quantity where marginal revenue is equal to marginal cost.

Because the demand curve has a kink, and the marginal revenue curve lies below the demand curve, the marginal revenue curve would have a gap where the two segments of the demand curve meet. That is, at the kink, or the profit maximizing price. Profit is maximized at the same price and quantity combination as long as the marginal cost curve crosses the marginal revenue curve anywhere within this gap. If variable costs change, a profit maximizing firm in oligopoly will not change price or quantity as long as the marginal cost curve crosses the marginal revenue curve within this gap.

The kinked demand curve model does not explain all behavior in oligopoly, but the gap in the marginal revenue curve helps to explain why firms in oligopoly change prices rather infrequently.

Prisoner's dilemma:

Game theory is a branch of mathematics often used in economics to explain strategic behavior. Prisoner's dilemma is a model in game theory that is used in economics to explain the behavior of firms in oligopoly.

Prisoner's dilemma explains why firms (without cooperating with competitors and without perfect knowledge of how their competitors will react, but knowing that their competitors will react in some fashion) will often find that the best strategy is the opposite strategy from what would be chosen if they could cooperate with the competition.

Why does this model have such a name? Why is it called prisoner's dilemma? The answer lies in the similarity of firms in oligopoly to the prisoners in the following story. Understanding this story may help to understand the strategy choices in the model of prisoner's dilemma for oligopoly.

The story goes like this:

Two people have been arrested for participating in the same crime. The police know that without a confession, not enough evidence exists to make a conviction. So the two prisoners are separated to prevent them from coordinating their stories. Each prisoner is then offered a deal in an attempt to generate a confession.

The deal offered is that if the prisoner confesses and is willing to testify against the other, he will go free as long as the other prisoner does not confess. If he refuses to confess, but the other prisoner does confess, he will face the maximum sentence. If they both confess, they will not go free but will face a reduced sentence. However, because of the weak evidence against them, they will both go free if neither confesses.

This story emphasizes the different strategy that will be selected because of the lack of perfect knowledge, the lack of cooperation. Because the prisoners are separated, each cannot know whether the other will confess or not. If they could collude, they would both choose not to confess, and both would be set free. But because they cannot collude, each would be likely to choose to confess in order to avoid the maximum sentence and retain the hope of being set free. As a result, each would choose to confess; neither would be set free, but neither would face the maximum sentence.

When the prisoner's dilemma model is applied to oligopoly, the strategic choices of firms will be similar to those of the prisoners in the above story. Each firm would be better off if the firms could cooperate, but would choose the opposite strategy if they cannot cooperate.

Prisoner's dilemma is a simplified model of oligopoly that focuses on only two firms, and the options available to these two firms. It can be modified to focus on one firm's decisions against "all competitors" in order to take into consideration the fact that a typical market will have more than two firms. Often, economics textbooks will use as an example the choice of whether or not to raise prices, or whether or not to spend money to advertise.

The main point of using the prisoner's dilemma as an explanation for behavior in oligopoly is that one strategy will be chosen based on competition while the opposite strategy will be chosen based on cooperation.

Cooperation in oligopoly:

The prisoner's dilemma model illustrates that firms in oligopoly can be better off if they are able to cooperate rather than compete. If they cooperate in the form of a secret agreement, this is called collusion. The practice of collusion is illegal in the United States and many other nations, but it is not illegal in all nations.

Cooperation might make firms better off, but at the same time it is likely to make consumers worse off. Cooperation often means higher prices and lower quantities for consumers. Cooperation also reduces the incentive for firms to develop new and improved products. This could lead to domestic industries losing out to foreign competitors who are not a party to any cooperative agreements.

One method that firms in oligopoly may use to cooperate is called price leadership. In the price leadership method, one firm changes its price, and other firms automatically match the price change. You can see a possible example of this in virtually every neighborhood in the United States. When one gas station changes its price, every other gas station in the same neighborhood will change to the exact same price on the same day.

Different strategies can be employed to determine which firm is the price leader. One is to have the largest firm set the price, and then other firms follow suit. This method appears to be useful in markets where one firm is a dominant firm. Other strategies include using the lowest-cost firm as the price leader, and having a barometric firm set the price for others to follow.

The barometric firm would be a firm that makes a public announcement, such as through a press release, of its intentions to change prices. In this public announcement, it will explain the reasons for a price change, such as trends in the costs of production. This would be a signal for other firms to match the price change.

Still another price leadership strategy would be for firms to hide their cooperation by using secret codes. They could agree to rotate the firm that is the price leader through a secret method in order to avoid having consumers and regulators know about this strategy. However, this strategy falls under the category of collusion that is likely to be illegal.

Price leadership eliminates the kink in the demand curve, since both price increases and price decreases will be followed. It also eliminates the prisoner's dilemma, since each firm will have knowledge of the strategy of the other firms.

One type of cooperation in oligopoly is known as a cartel. A cartel is an organization of firms in an industry that agrees to restrict competition between its members in order to maximize the profits of the entire organization. All members of a cartel agree formally or informally to set prices and / or output levels as if the cartel were a monopoly.

An international cartel is a cartel composed of firms from different countries.

Since profits are maximized for the cartel as a unit, and not for individual firms in a cartel, an incentive to cheat exists. If one firm in a cartel can find a way to secretly break the agreement, such as by selling more output at a lower price, that firm will be able to increase its profits over what it could make within the agreement. This would decrease the profits of the cartel as a unit. Such cheating can easily break up the cartel, especially if the cheating is detected; all firms would then be made worse off. Enforcement of agreements is the key to avoid cheating that will break up a cartel. Because of the incentive to cheat, most cartels are not successful for very long. The conditions necessary for a successful cartel include few firms in the industry, significant barriers to entry, identical products, few opportunities for secret actions, and no legal barriers to sharing agreements.

Cartels are generally illegal in the United States and many other countries. However, international cartels are not illegal. The most well-known cartel, OPEC (the organization of petroleum exporting countries), is an international cartel whose enforcement mechanism is aided by the fact that its firms are actually the countries themselves rather than private organizations.

Even in the United States, where cartels are illegal, some cartel-like organizations are endorsed by the government. The NCAA (National Collegiate Athletic Association) is a cartel of colleges and universities with a governing board that sets and enforces rules. Congress has granted Major League Baseball a special exemption to antitrust laws in order to allow it to function as a cartel.

Monopoly:

Monopoly is a market structure in which one firm supplies the entire market. The product supplied has no close substitutes. The market size can be large or small. A firm in a monopoly market structure is called a monopolist.

Because there is only one firm in the market, the firm's demand curve is the same as the market demand curve. Unlike a firm in perfect competition, a monopolist is a price maker. It decides the price at which to sell its product. It also decides what quantity to offer for sale. A monopolist has market power.

How does a monopolist set its price and quantity? It is not true that a monopolist can continually raise its prices, with each price increase necessarily increasing the monopolist's profits. It is also not true that a monopolist always earns a profit. A monopolist has costs just like any other firm, and must earn revenue in excess of these costs in order to earn a profit.

The demand curve faced by a monopolist is downward sloping. This means that it can only increase output if it lowers its price. It cannot lower its price only on any additional output that it wishes to sell, however. It must lower its price on all units sold, including the units that it could sell at a higher price. If a monopolist raises its price, the downward sloping demand curve means that it will sell fewer units. The exception to this is in the case of price discrimination, which will be discussed later in this chapter.

By having to lower the price on all units instead of just the additional units, the marginal revenue curve lies below the demand curve. Like any firm in any market structure, profits are maximized at the quantity of output where marginal revenue (MR) is equal to marginal cost (MC). With the marginal revenue curve below the demand curve, this quantity will be lower than the profit-maximizing quantity in perfect competition. Since the monopolist sets the quantity where MR=MC, supply is determined by marginal cost.

Also, unlike perfect competition, marginal revenue is not equal to price in a monopoly. Profits are maximized at the quantity where MR=MC, but at this quantity the monopolist can charge the price where this quantity intersects the demand curve. Since the demand curve lies above the marginal revenue curve, this price will be higher than what would occur under perfect competition. The profit-maximizing quantity corresponds to the marginal cost curve but the profit-maximizing price corresponds to the demand curve. Since the price is set by the demand curve, and price also equals average revenue in the absence of price discrimination, the average revenue curve is the demand curve.

All else equal, then, the monopolist will sell a lower quantity at a higher price than what would occur under perfect competition.

With the output quantity determined by the marginal revenue curve, and the price determined by the demand curve (which lies above the marginal revenue curve), a monopolist doesn't really have a supply curve. It has a supply point. This is because only one point in a graph factors in price, quantity, demand, and marginal revenue.

A monopolist that sells a product with an inelastic demand can set a price higher than a monopolist that sells a product with an elastic demand, all else equal. This means that a monopoly for a product that is deemed to be a necessity, which would likely be highly inelastic, is of special concern to the public and to policy makers.

Why do monopolies exist? A monopoly exists because the barriers to entry into the market are prohibitive. These barriers prevent other firms from entering the market. Since other firms are not able to enter the market to take advantage of profit potential, it is possible for a monopolist to earn economic profits in the long run. These barriers to entry can be divided into three general classes: natural barriers, anti-competitive behavior, and government-created monopolies.

Natural barriers:

Economies of scale would be a natural barrier that would create a monopoly. If the entire market demand can be met on the downward sloping portion of the long run average total cost curve, then one firm can supply the entire market at a lower cost than two or more competing firms could. Splitting the market between firms would mean operating at a scale with higher costs. Economies of scale typically involve high startup costs, high fixed costs, and lower variable costs per unit of output. An example of a monopoly due to economies of scale would be a plant that generates electricity for a local market. A monopoly created by natural barriers is called a natural monopoly.

Economies of scale can offset the efficiency gains from a perfectly competitive market which does not allow for economies of scale. This is why the discussion about a monopolist charging a higher price for a lower quantity relative to a competitive firm included the disclaimer "all else equal".

Anti-competitive behavior:

A firm that has gained market power may engage in activities that are designed to keep competitors out of the market. For example, an established firm can afford to lower its price below the break-even price in the short run whenever a start-up firm threatens to take over some of the market share. A start-up firm would not have the resources needed to survive if it were forced to compete with prices that are substantially lower than costs. After the competition is eliminated, the monopolist will then raise its prices again to maximize profits.

A monopolist may be able to keep out competition by buying up a key resource. If nobody else has access to a key resource, then no competition can exist. For example, if a monopolist produces a product that can only be manufactured using a specific natural resource, the monopolist may attempt to buy all the land where this resource is known to exist.

Anti-competitive behavior is generally illegal under antitrust laws. However, small local monopolies can often "fly under the radar", and avoid government scrutiny. For example, in a small town with only one restaurant, the restaurant may temporarily lower its prices or even raise wages in order to prevent a competing restaurant from being successful. The government may not be willing to use its resources to catch all such violators.

Government-created monopolies:

Government action can also create monopolies. Patent laws provide monopoly protection for the owners of patents for a period of time, which in the United States is currently 17 years. Governments can also issue licenses for certain products that guarantee a monopoly or contract for services in which the government is the only buyer.

Because a monopolist sells a lower quantity at a higher price, all else equal, than a firm in perfect competition, the monopoly market structure is considered to be inefficient. Recall from the discussion of perfect competition, which is considered to be the most efficient market structure, that efficiency is defined by total surplus. Total surplus is maximized under perfect competition, and includes the entire area left of the equilibrium point lying both below the demand curve and above the supply curve.

Consumer surplus is the portion of total surplus that lies above the market price. Producer surplus is the portion of total surplus that lies below the market price. For a monopolist, the same graph would have the marginal cost curve substitute for the supply curve. This allows for comparison of surplus between the two market structures. The monopolist would have a higher price and lower output than would exist under perfect competition. The area of total surplus is lower under a monopoly than under perfect competition by the area bordered by the monopolist's price and output point, the point where this quantity intersects the marginal cost curve, and the price and output point under perfect competition. This triangular area represents loss of total efficiency, and is called deadweight loss. Also, the area of the remaining total surplus under monopoly that lies between the monopolist's price and the price under perfect competition represents surplus that is transferred from the consumer to the producer. The net result is that a monopoly market structure will have a lower consumer surplus (consumers are worse off), a higher producer surplus (sellers are better off), and a lower total surplus, resulting in less efficiency.

Price discrimination:

In general, a firm cannot lower its price on some units sold without lowering its price on all units sold, even the units that it could sell at a higher price. Otherwise, the customers that pay the lower price will simply sell the product to the customers who would be charged the higher price. This would prevent the firm from making sales at the higher price. Under certain conditions, though, a firm may be able to charge different prices to different customers based on willingness to pay. It could increase revenue without increasing

76

cost, and therefore increase profit by doing so. If the firm can identify different classes of buyers, with different demand curves with different elasticity, and at the same time prevent the resale of its product, it can gain by using price discrimination.

Examples of price discrimination in the real world:

Airlines charge higher prices during the times and dates when business travel is highest. Business customers have a lower price elasticity of demand than other customers.

Restaurants, theaters, and other businesses often give senior citizen discounts to a class of customers that includes many people on a smaller budget (think fixed income) than the general population.

In-state tuition, grocery coupons, and lower prices for larger (bulk) purchases are other forms of price discrimination.

Market Failure

Perhaps it will help to avoid misconceptions about the term market failure as it applies to the study of economics if we start with a definition:

Market failure: When the free market does not allocate resources to their most efficient uses.

Market failure does not occur just because somebody doesn't agree with the outcome of free markets. That would be a normative issue. Economic thinking requires dealing with positive, not normative issues.

Market failure involves the concept of externalities. Externalities occur when actions of producers or consumers affect third parties: people not involved in the production, purchase, or sale of a particular good. Externalities are sometimes referred to as spillovers. Externalities can be positive or negative. An externality can be a spillover benefit or a spillover cost.

A few more relevant definitions:

Private benefit: A benefit received by a party to a transaction.
Private cost: A cost paid by a party to a transaction.
Social benefit: Total benefit of a transaction: private benefit plus external benefit.
Social cost: Total cost of a transaction: private cost plus external cost.

Flu vaccinations would be an example of a positive externality. Each year, many people receive flu vaccinations. The private cost is paid by the individuals receiving the vaccinations (or their insurance companies). The private benefit is the lower health risk and the associated gain in peace of mind for the individuals receiving the vaccinations. While many people are involved in these transactions, many others are not. For a variety of reasons, many people choose not to receive this vaccination. Those who do not receive the vaccination still receive a benefit. As more people receive flu vaccinations, it becomes less likely that those who choose not to receive vaccinations will be exposed to the flu. The general health of the population benefits from flu vaccinations, not just those individuals who pay to receive them.

With a positive externality, the free market price and quantity does not factor in all of the benefits. Resources are under-allocated. Too little production of the good in question occurs. The free market price and quantity will be determined by the equilibrium where the supply and demand curves intersect, based only on private benefits and costs. If all of the social benefits were included, the demand curve would be farther to the right, creating equilibrium with a higher price and a higher quantity.

Air pollution would be an example of a negative externality. If the unregulated production of a particular good involves polluting the air, this production imposes a social cost that is not factored into the market price and quantity of the good being produced. The market price and quantity will be determined by the private costs and benefits only. The social costs of air pollution are many: poor health for residents and animal life; increased medical expenses; shorter life expectancies; missed work and production due to illness. Even obscured scenery is a social cost.

With a negative externality, resources are over-allocated. Too much production of the good in question occurs. If all of the social costs were included, the market supply curve would be farther to the left, resulting in a higher price and a lower quantity.

The socially optimal level of an externality is not necessarily zero. In the example of the flu vaccinations, a solution that involves every single person in the population receiving a vaccine may indeed add in a cost that exceeds the social benefit. In the example of air pollution, a law that requires firms to emit zero pollution may force firms to shut down, resulting in no production. Shutting down production may very well involve social costs in excess of the social costs caused by air pollution.

Possible solutions to the problems of externalities:

For positive externalities: The government could pay a subsidy to consumers who purchase the good. This would mean that the cost to consumers would be less than the amount received by producers. If the amount of the subsidy is the amount that would induce enough demand to equal the socially optimal level of production, then this would have the effect of shifting the demand curve to the right. This would result in the socially optimal level of production at the socially optimal price. Efficient allocation of resources would result.

The problems with this solution: No market exists to determine what level of production is socially optimal. That level requires some guesswork, and the result would be rather arbitrary. Also, government-paid subsidies involve problems relating to the methods that governments have for financing expenditures. Those problems will be discussed in later chapters.

For negative externalities: Three possible solutions for negative externalities are a tax on production, a government command, and marketable permits.

Tax on production: A tax for a negative externality has the opposite effect as that of a subsidy for a positive externality. A tax on production will increase the cost of production of the good in question, resulting in a leftward shift in the supply curve. If the tax is set at the proper level, the result would be the socially optimal level of production at the socially optimal price. Efficient allocation of resources would result.

The problem with this solution: No market exists to determine the socially optimal level of production. Guesswork is involved, which would produce rather arbitrary results. One added benefit for the government would be additional tax revenue.

Government command: Instead of imposing a tax on a negative externality, the government could pass laws setting the legal upper limits on the amount of the negative externality that is produced.

The problems with this solution: The limit would not be market-based; it would instead be somewhat arbitrary. Those who create the negative externality would have no incentive to lower the production of the negative beyond the legal limit. With a tax, a firm would have an incentive to find new technology that would lower the tax along with the externality. With a government command, no such incentive exists. A command will not necessarily lead to an efficient allocation of resources.

Marketable permits (also known as cap and trade): Cap and trade is a system that is designed to eliminate many of the problems associated with the tax and the government command methods for decreasing a negative externality. It is the only method of the three that uses actual market forces to determine the amount of a negative externality that is produced by any individual firm. Cap and trade works like this: The government sets a limit on the maximum amount of a negative externality that will be allowed, but this limit is on an entire industry instead of an individual firm. The government then issues permits for the negative externality. The total permits issued equal the maximum externality that is allowed. Any individual firm can produce as much of the externality as it wishes, as long as it has enough permits to cover that amount. If a firm wants to produce more of the negative externality than it has permits for, it can only do so if it buys more permits from other firms in the industry. The total of the externality is controlled by the government industry-wide, but the market for permits determines the amount of the externality produced by individual firms. The permits will have their own market, and their market price will create an incentive for firms to reduce production of the negative externality.

The market for permits could also be used to reduce the industry-wide amount of a negative externality. For example, an environmental group could decide to purchase permits with no intention of producing the externality. By holding permits, the environmental group could prevent the permits from being used by firms that would produce the externality.

Economic Systems

Modern economies are generally classified as either market economies or command economies. Economies that have elements of both market economies and command economies are called mixed economies.

Because every world economy today does have some elements of both market economies and command economies, they are all technically mixed economies. Since this provides no distinction between economies that in reality are vastly different from one another, economies that have mostly market economy features are considered to be market economies, and economies that have mostly command economy features are considered to be command economies.

What follows is a summary of the major features of a market economy, the major features of a command economy, and how a mixed economy differs from each.

In a market economy, the private sector is the principle component of the economy. Characteristics of a market economy include private ownership of land and other means of production; private ownership of businesses; individual and firm decision-making; risk and reward for risk-taking; job availability dependent upon economic conditions; worker compensation based on contributions to efficiency and output, creating incentives for innovation, hard work, education, and entrepreneurship; market forces provide efficiency; equality of opportunity is a common goal. An economic system based on a market economy is called capitalism.

In a command economy, the public sector is the principle component of the economy. Characteristics of a command economy include no private ownership of land; limited private ownership of property; businesses are state-owned; workers are employees of the state; workers are guaranteed jobs, with little incentive for hard work; businesses have little incentive for efficiency and innovation; consumer choices are limited; prices and output are often set by the state rather than market forces, creating shortages; rationing occurs via long lines, quantity limits on purchases, and a black market where incentives exist for corruption. Command economies are often associated with socialism, where equality of outcome is a goal.

The terms "command economy", "socialism", and "communism" are often confused with one another, or are treated as being interchangeable. Actually, there are distinctions. A command economy is an economy with the features listed above. Socialism is pretty much the same, but with a narrower definition: socialism is an economic system that is characterized by state ownership and control of the means of production and the distribution of output. Communism is different. Communism is a political philosophy that uses a socialist economic system as part of its philosophy. Communism requires socialism as a step in the development of society. In order to advance the philosophy, it mandates a socialist economy.

A mixed economy, as defined above, will have major aspects of both market and command economies. These take many different forms. In general, they would involve economies where large segments are left alone for market forces to work, while other large segments are controlled by the government for various reasons, such as national interest and national security.

Governments exert some influence over every type of economy, so market economies all have some areas where market forces alone do not determine economic outcomes. Government involvement influences economic decisions by such means as government-provided infrastructure; government regulations of businesses and industries; tax decisions, especially taxes that are targeted towards specific industries (think sin tax); subsidies of specific industries; trade restrictions; which groups to tax by how much; which groups to give transfer payments to; antitrust laws; environmental laws; and in many other ways.

Market forces exert some influence even in command economies, and this trend is growing. Countries with command economies are finding more and more over time that they cannot contain market forces, and that it is not desirable to do so, especially in remote rural areas. So they have started allowing private businesses to develop in specific areas, along with allowing more private economic decisions and incentives.

A market economy does not depend on a democratic form of government for its existence. A market economy can exist even with a dictatorship. However, the incentive for interference is great when any person or group of people have centralized political power, so that a market economy with a more decentralized form of government is more likely to survive over time. In times of national emergency, when quick action is required, a powerful central government, with few bureaucratic snags in the system, can be more effective than a democracy, where decision-making is more decentralized. But such situations may require government interference in economic decision-making. Since this often results in a transfer of economic power, dictatorships may be reluctant to return the economic power to the control of market forces once the emergency situation has passed.

As stated earlier, all modern economies tend to have varying degrees of mixed economy elements. Each nation tends to be unique in the details. Changes in the economies of nations occur rather frequently in response to economic and political events.

Money and Banking Basics

The related topics of money and banking in the study of economics involve concepts and issues that are complex and often politically controversial. This book covers only the basic concepts and terminology typically found in an introductory economics or macroeconomics textbook. I consider an understanding of these basics to be a prerequisite for the more complex aspects of these topics, and at the same time useful information for students and non-students alike. Some of these basics involve concepts that are widely misunderstood by members of the general public.

The details of the topics of money and banking differ from country to country, from one economy to another. In order to avoid the confusion that would result from an attempt to mention all of these differences at the same time as the concepts are introduced, the discussion here is based on the system in the United States, including the US dollar and the Federal Reserve System.

Money:

The definitions that different people use for money are somewhat arbitrary. Economists classify money into different categories, or measures. These measures are: M-1, M-2, M-3, and L; they are described below. The distinction between these measures can be somewhat unclear. However, a simple definition of money would look something like this:

Money: anything that is widely accepted as payment in exchange for goods and services.

In order to understand the functions that money serve, consider the alternative, which is a barter economy. A barter economy depends on what is called a coincidence of wants. This means that if you want something that someone else has to offer, in order to get it you must give that person something that they want. Usually, that person is not going to want whatever it is that you have to offer. You will have to find a third person, and probably involve many more people, before you can find an equilibrium where everybody involved will get something that they want in exchange for something that they have to offer.

If you want or have something that is perishable or decreases in value over time, finding someone to trade with becomes a very urgent process. This entire process is very cumbersome and time-consuming. People would end up spending so much of their time just dealing with activities related to making exchanges that they would have little time left to actually be producing something. It is very difficult to imagine a barter economy that has any kind of economic growth, let alone any advances in technology or even education.

Involving many people in the many transactions that would be required so that everybody gets what they want can involve thousands of different goods and services. This would require some sort of exchange rate between all of the goods and services in order to know what the relative values are. It would be very difficult for anybody to keep track of all of the different exchange rates for all of the different combinations of goods and services that can be traded for each other.

In addition, you have to consider the source of the goods or services that you have to offer. You could work for someone, and use whatever they pay you for exchanges. Your employer won't likely pay you by giving you all of the goods and services that you want. They would have to have everything that each and every employee wants in order to do that. And they won't pay you with what you want at exactly the same time that you want it. You would want to spread your earnings out between pay days, even save some to increase your wealth and make larger purchases in the future.

Economists have identified three functions that money serves to distinguish a money economy from a barter economy: medium of exchange, unit of account, and store of value.

Medium of exchange: Money serves as a means of payment. It eliminates the necessity of a coincidence of wants present in a barter economy.

Unit of account: This is a standard of value, or a common denominator, to measure the material worth of all goods and services available in the economy against each other. This gives people a general idea of the relative values of the items that they frequently purchase. This keeps people from having to know what the exchange rates are between thousands, or potentially millions, of goods and services.

Store of value: Money allows people to store purchasing power. This is necessary because the time that income is received will not always coincide with the time that people will want to use the money to finance expenditures.

As noted above, money is divided into different categories, or measures. Perhaps it would be helpful to list the assets that are included in each measure of money at this time. This might help with understanding the brief discussion that follows:

Measures of money:

M-1 includes currency and coins (cash money) held by the public; demand deposits (checking accounts); traveler's checks and other checkable deposits such as NOW accounts; ATS accounts; and credit union share-draft balances.

M-2 includes everything defined as M-1, plus overnight RPs issued by commercial banks; overnight Eurodollar deposits; money market mutual fund shares (general purpose); savings deposits at all depository institutions; small time deposits (less than $100,000) at all depository institutions; and money market deposit accounts.

M-3 includes everything defined as M-2, plus large time deposits at all depository institutions ($100,000 or more); term RPs; term Eurodollar deposits; and money market mutual fund shares (institutions).

L includes everything defined as M-3, plus banker's acceptances, commercial paper, savings bonds, and short term U.S. Treasury securities (T-Bills).

A few notes concerning money:

The distinctions made with these various measures can be somewhat arbitrary; they are mostly based on the relative liquidity of the different classifications of money. Liquidity means the relative ease with which something can be converted to cash.

Many people think of money in terms of only currency and coins. Currency and coins issued by the government are considered legal tender, meaning that no seller can legally refuse to accept currency and coins as payment for goods and services. However, currency and coins comprise a relatively small fraction of all money. Demand deposits (more commonly known as checking accounts) make up about 80% of M-1 money.

Currency (paper money) at one point in time could be legally exchanged for a specific amount of a commodity such as gold or silver. This was called the gold standard (or the silver standard). Coins were made of these commodities, and were called commodity money. This means that the coins had a value based on the material that they were composed of, separate from the face value of the coins. This meant that if the value of the gold or silver that the coins were made of exceeded the face value of the coins, people would tend to hoard them. This would reduce the amount of money in circulation, and reduce economic activity. This tendency to hoard commodity money is called Gresham's Law. Supply and demand forces, including hoarding, would tend to keep the values of the commodity in line with the face value of the coins. At least in theory, commodity money would mean that inflation would be low but economic growth could be limited. Depending on the school of thought, economic downturns could be more common and more severe.

Currency and coins no longer have value based on commodity prices. The value of cash money is based on the faith that people put in it. This is closely related to the stability of the government. Money that is not backed by commodities is called fiduciary, or fiat, money. One advantage of using fiduciary money is that it is much less expensive for the government to issue it. The government does not have to use or pledge valuable resources such as gold and silver. One disadvantage is that with fiduciary money, the government may tend to issue too much of it, which could create inflation.

I won't go into detail to describe everything in the above list of the measures of money. Many of these items rarely need additional explanations for economics class. M-1 is called transaction money. It includes forms of money that are generally used to finance transactions. By far the largest form of money is demand deposits, not currency and coins. Currency and coins held at financial institutions (such as banks) and by the government is not part of the money supply. Only currency and coins held by the public (in circulation) are counted as money.

M-1 is the most widely-used measure of money, especially by those who want to emphasize the medium of exchange function of money.

Banking:

Different countries throughout the world use different banking systems. There are differences based on different government structures, different levels of industrialization, degree of globalization, even different cultures and religions.

Banking systems have been undergoing many major changes in recent years. New technologies are being used. International banking is growing and evolving. Global currencies, such as the U.S. dollar and the Euro, have increasingly influenced world banking operations. Even within the United States, a relaxation of banking regulations is changing the fundamental ways that the banking system operates.

The purpose here is not to provide details of all of these differences and changes. Instead, the focus is on one of the basics of the United States banking system: How commercial banks create money.

Banks act as financial intermediaries. They use funds deposited by savers to make loans to borrowers. Banks make profit from this activity. They charge a higher interest rate to borrowers than they pay to savers.

In the United States, the Federal Reserve System (The Fed) supervises commercial banks. The Fed sets rules for commercial banks based on the Fed's monetary policy. In addition, the Fed provides services to commercial banks. The Fed provides currency for banks, makes loans to banks, holds reserves for banks, and clears checks between banks. The Fed has been called a banker's bank because of these services.

How Banks Create Money:

When people deposit money in a commercial bank in the United States, the amount deposited remains part of the U.S. money supply. Checking accounts are part of the M-1 definition of money. Savings accounts are generally considered to be part of the M-2 definition of money. Depositors can withdraw their funds on demand. This creates an equal liability for the banks. The funds that the banks accept in deposits belong to the depositors. The deposits are called reserves for the banks.

On a typical day, only a very small fraction of the deposits in a bank will be needed to meet the demand for withdrawals. The bank will attempt to keep enough currency on hand to meet the demand for currency transactions. The rest of the deposits are kept at the Fed for safekeeping. It is not profitable for banks to have a lot of reserves sitting around, not earning any income. So banks loan out the reserves to borrowers and charge interest on the loans. These loans decrease the amount of reserves for the banks.

Banks cannot loan out all of the money that is deposited. Each bank must keep enough reserves on hand to meet the daily needs for withdrawals. The Fed determines the level of reserves that banks are required to hold. This level is a percentage of total deposits. This level is called the required reserve ratio, or the reserve requirement. The Fed determines the reserve requirement based on its monetary policy. Since this ratio will help determine the size of the money supply, the reserve requirement becomes a tool that the Fed uses in its monetary policy.

Since banks cannot loan out 100% of its reserves, this type of banking system is called a fractional reserve system. The reserves for an individual bank above the reserve requirement are called excess reserves. An individual commercial bank is allowed to loan out money as long as it has excess reserves. When a bank makes a loan from its excess reserves, it typically will credit funds to the borrower's account, which is part of the money supply. The reserves that provided the loan, however, are still counted as deposits in other customers' accounts, which are also part of the money supply. So when banks make loans, they increase the money supply. Money is created "out of thin air".

For each deposit, an individual bank is allowed to loan out, and increase the money supply by, an amount equal to:

(Amount of the deposit) times (1 minus the reserve requirement)

Relatively widespread misconceptions exist about the amount of this expansion of the money supply, so I will clarify with an example. If the reserve requirement is 10%, then banks will be allowed to loan out, in total, an amount equal to $90 for every $100 dollars on deposit. This would be $100 times (1 - 0.1), using the formula above. Many people incorrectly believe that a bank with a 10% reserve requirement can loan out 10 times the amount of the deposit, or $1000 for every $100 on deposit. This greatly overstates the ability of an individual bank to increase the money supply, and the effects of the fractional reserve system on the overall economy.

However, that is for individual banks. When an individual bank makes a loan from excess reserves, it sets off a chain of events throughout the entire banking system, which multiplies the amount of money that eventually can be created out of that initial transaction. The money supply in the entire economy, in the entire banking system, can expand by more than the amount created by an initial deposit in an individual bank. A typical borrower does not borrow money in order to leave it sitting in a bank account. The borrowed money is spent or invested in the economy. This becomes income for somebody else. To the extent that this new income is then deposited into an account at a different commercial bank within the banking system, reserves are created at that other bank. The other bank can in turn loan out its excess reserves. This process then can repeat itself continuously, increasing the money supply with every additional loan.

The maximum amount that an initial deposit can increase the money supply within the entire banking system is given by the formula:

Deposit expansion multiplier = 1 / reserve requirement

In the above example, an initial deposit of $100 with a 10% reserve requirement allowed the bank where the deposit is held to increase the money supply by $90. If you apply that same $100 deposit to the deposit expansion multiplier, the entire banking system would be able to increase the money supply by $1000 ($100 initial deposit times the deposit expansion multiplier, which is 1 / 0.1).

The incorrect assumption mentioned above, about the ability of one bank to increase the money supply, actually is the same amount as the true maximum amount that the money supply can eventually be increased by within the entire banking system. Economics classes in Money and Banking and Macroeconomics often require students to be able to make calculations based on this formula. Keep in mind, however, that this formula is only a mathematical maximum. The actual amount of money that would be created within a real world banking system would be somewhat less than the maximum amount.

The reason why the real world expansion of the money supply would be less than the mathematical maximum calculated using the deposit expansion multiplier formula: It is not realistic to assume that every individual bank would always keep its excess reserves at exactly zero. That would be required for the money supply to increase by the maximum amount. Not all loan proceeds are deposited in the borrowers' accounts, although most would be. When these loan proceeds are spent, they do not always end up as deposits in another bank. Also, excess reserves at a given bank are not only increased by deposits, they are also decreased by withdrawals, which we can assume occur daily in each bank.

Measuring the Economy

National income accounting is a system of measurements which allows for comparisons of the sizes of different economies, as well as measurements of one economy's performance over time. These are measurements of an economy's output and income on a macroeconomic level.

Given the wide variety of goods and services produced in a modern economy, the total output cannot be measured simply by adding together the number of units produced. Different goods and services have different values, so national income accounting requires measuring the value of production. The most common measure is Gross Domestic Product, which is commonly shortened to GDP. The definition of GDP:

Gross Domestic Product (GDP) is the market value of all final goods and services produced in a year within a country's borders.

This definition necessarily excludes any production that is not traded on legal markets. For example, housework performed by a paid housekeeper would be counted, while the same work performed by household members for no pay would not be counted. If no measurable payment for services is included, it doesn't count. Transactions on the black market, such as illegal drug transactions, are not legally recognized or accurately measurable, and are therefore excluded. These exclusions mean that the official GDP calculations understate actual production.

Only final goods and services (those available to the ultimate consumer) are counted. This avoids double-counting, since the value of final goods and services incorporates the cost of intermediate goods. Intermediate goods are goods that are used in the production of other goods. GDP can be computed by counting each stage of production, but only if the value added at each stage is counted, and not the total value of the output at each stage.

Production is counted in GDP in the year it is produced, regardless of when it is sold. If a sale takes place in a later year, the later year's GDP will only reflect the income earned at the time of the sale, not the full value of the good being sold. The value of used goods sold is not included, since it does not represent the current year's production.

The method used for including unsold production in GDP is to measure changes in inventories. Inventory is production that has not been sold. Within the categories of expenditures for the computation of GDP, an increase in inventory would be investment while a decrease in inventory would be consumption.

The Circular Flow Model:

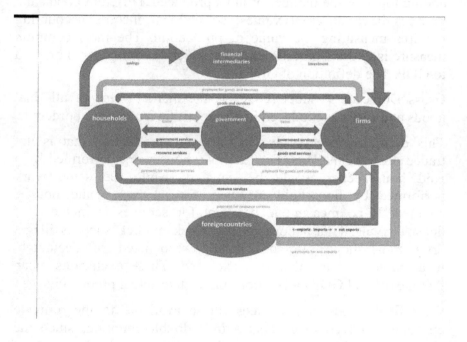

Economics classes and textbooks always seem to begin the discussion of national income accounting with a detailed look at the circular flow model. They generally start with a basic model with unrealistic assumptions of a closed economy with no government, in order to highlight the relationships between households and firms, and then gradually add in the other segments. I don't necessarily agree with this approach. I understand why it is done this way: an understanding of the relationships is important for an understanding of what national income accounting measures. I just find that this approach is confusing for many students, especially whenever the intermediate models are used for exercises and test questions. I believe that other methods could be used to highlight the interrelationships involved. My approach here is sort of a compromise. I have included a diagram of a circular flow model (above), but only the final, complete version, not the intermediate ones that gradually add in segments of the economy. Also, I will not include a detailed explanation of the circular flow model. Students can get that directly from their textbooks or other class materials, if required. I will just give a brief description of the important points to be learned from this model.

The circular flow model shows that a national economy is a system. Income and output flow between segments of the economy. The total economy can be measured as income, and it also can be measured as output.

The orange lines in the above model represent flows of income; the blue lines represent flows of output, or non-cash flows within the model. The model shows that these flows (except for leakages and injections mentioned below) stay within the system: the arrows show the direction of the flows. For example, an employee of a firm will offer his services for pay. The employee represents the household sector. His services are not cash flows, they are labor. This is represented by the blue arrow going from households to firms, labeled resource services. But the pay that he receives for this labor is income in the form of wages. This is a flow of money, and it is represented by the orange arrow going from firms to households.

The international sector is represented by lines that are not arrows. This is done for simplicity purposes. The model could show one set of arrows to represent exports and another set of arrows to represent imports. To keep from filling the model with too many arrows, these are simply shown as lines to represent net exports. Since net exports can be either positive or negative, the model doesn't show arrows to indicate a direction of flow.

Financial intermediaries are not segments of the economy. They are shown to indicate that money that flows into them (called savings) is a leakage in the system. Money that flows out of them and back into the system (called investment) is an injection in the system. In equilibrium, leakages would equal injections.

That is all that I intend to include about the circular flow model. I only want to highlight the relationships that you need for an understanding of the discussion to follow.

Gross Domestic Product or GDP:

The circular flow model shows the interrelationship between the four sectors of the economy: households, firms, government, and the international sector. Since GDP is a measure of production for the entire economy, it can be measured by adding together the expenditures for production of each of these four components, or sectors. Using this method to compute GDP is called the expenditures approach. The expenditures approach uses a formula that should become familiar to all students of macroeconomics:

$GDP = C + I + G + NX$

Where:

C = Consumption, or expenditures by the household sector

I = Gross Private Domestic Investment, or expenditures by the firms (or business sector)

G = Government purchases of goods and services, or expenditures by the government sector

NX = Net Exports, or expenditures by the international sector

Note that G does not include all government spending, but only spending on purchases of goods and services. Total government spending also includes transfer payments, or payments for such things as unemployment compensation, welfare payments, and Social Security benefits. These transfer payments are not included in GDP because they do not represent current production in the economy. They only represent the transfer of money from one segment of the economy to another.

Net exports (NX) equals total exports minus total imports. Exports are added into GDP because they represent goods and services that are produced within the economy but are not part of domestic expenditures. Imports are subtracted because they represent spending on goods and services that were not produced within the economy. Often this definition of net exports is reflected in the formula that you see for GDP, so that the formula looks like this:

$$GDP = C + I + G + (X\text{-}M)$$

In this version of the formula, net exports is represented by "(X-M)" instead of "NX" as in the other version of the formula. Also, sometimes "NX" is written simply as "X", and students need to be aware that this X is different from the X in (X-M).

Often for economics class you will be given a list of different values and be asked to calculate GDP based on the numbers on the list. GDP is easier to calculate using the expenditures approach than it is using the income approach (discussed in the next section of this chapter) because the expenditures approach includes fewer categories of numbers, and the ones used are generally more straight-forward and easier to remember.

The formula using the expenditures approach, $GDP = C + I + G + X$, is something that is much easier to remember than the formula for the income approach.

GDP Using the Income Approach:

First, a quick reference formula:

Compensation of employees (wages) plus net interest plus rent plus profits (proprietors' income plus corporate profits)

Equals

National income (NI)

Plus

Indirect business taxes (sales tax plus excise tax)

Equals

Net national product (NNP)

Plus

Capital consumption allowance (depreciation)

Equals

Gross national product (GNP)

Minus

Net factor income from abroad (net foreign factor income, which is income received by citizens outside the nation's borders minus income received by foreigners within the nation's borders).

Equals

Gross domestic product (GDP)

The previous section showed how to calculate GDP using the expenditures approach. If you recall from the circular flow model, the flow of expenditures in the economy has a corresponding flow of income. Since these flows are equal in equilibrium, Gross Domestic Product, or GDP, can also be computed from the incomes received by the factors of production. This method of computing GDP is called the income approach.

Recall that the income received by the factors of production is as follows:

Labor earns wages (sometimes called compensation of employees); capital earns interest; and land earns rent. Also, firms earn profits, which remain within the circular flow. Sometimes, economists consider entrepreneurship to be a separate factor of production (rather than a special category of labor), and profit would be listed as the income received by entrepreneurs. Profit as an income category is in turn divided into two categories: proprietors' income (sole proprietorships and partnerships) and corporate profits (corporations).

Total income received by the segments of the economy, then, would be:

Wages + Interest + Rent + Profits

This sum of income received by the segments of the economy does not add up to GDP, however, and will not match the GDP amount that is calculated by using the expenditures approach. Some adjustments need to be made in order to get from this number to

GDP. This number does have a name, however: National Income, or NI. It follows that the formula for national income is:

NI = Wages + Interest + Rent + Proprietors' Income + Corporate Profits

From national income, three more adjustments are needed in order to get to GDP.

First, you may notice that government receipts are not part of this equation. This is because income tax receipts include money that is part of the incomes of the other segments of the economy. They are already being counted elsewhere. However, some taxes are collected from consumers by businesses, which have to turn this money over to the government. These taxes include state and local sales taxes, and excise taxes. Together, they are called indirect business taxes. In order to balance income and expenditures, this amount needs to be added to NI. This yields a number that is called net national product, or NNP.

NNP = NI + Indirect Business Taxes

This number (NNP) still does not equal GDP, because GDP using the expenditures approach includes an item called "gross private domestic investment". Some of this amount is not received as income. Some of it is used to replace worn-out equipment, plus the replacement of damaged or accidentally destroyed equipment. This replacement value is called capital consumption allowance. The routine replacement of worn-out equipment is called depreciation, and is computed and allocated over the lifetime of the equipment using an accounting procedure at each individual firm. Since depreciation makes up the vast majority of the capital consumption allowance, often this allowance is simply referred to as depreciation. In order to balance income and expenditures, this amount needs to be added to income. Adding the capital consumption allowance (or depreciation) to NNP will yield a number that is called Gross National Product, or GNP.

GNP = NNP + Capital Consumption Allowance (or Depreciation)

Notice the distinction in terms here: GNP, NNP. The difference is gross vs. net. Gross refers to gross investment and net refers to net investment, which is total investment net of the allowance for depreciation. You may need this information for exercises in economics class. The formula is:

Gross investment minus depreciation equals net investment.

Okay, we are almost there, but not quite. We are looking for GDP, and we now have GNP. GNP includes income received by citizens, regardless of whether the income was earned on production within the country or not. It excludes income earned within the country's borders by non-citizens. GDP is a measure of production that occurs within a nation's borders, regardless of the nationality of those who produce it. An adjustment needs to be made to GNP to account for this difference. This adjustment is called net factor income from abroad, or net foreign factor income. It is found by taking income received by citizens outside the nation's borders, and subtracting income received by foreigners within the nation's borders. Subtracting net factor income from abroad will yield GDP. Finally!!

GDP = GNP - Net Factor Income from Abroad

This GDP amount, found using the income approach, should be equal to GDP using the expenditures approach. Since compilation of figures in the real world is imperfect, there may be a difference for routine error and rounding.

This explanation of the income approach to calculating GDP is rather lengthy. It begins with income received by the factors of production, makes several adjustments, and ends up with an amount equal to GDP. Perhaps what you are looking for is a summary or a formula instead of the lengthy explanation. For that reason, I have included a summary above and again here:

GDP = Wages (compensation of employees) + Interest + Rent + Profits (proprietors' income plus corporate profits) - Net Factor Income from Abroad + Capital Consumption Allowance (depreciation) + Indirect Business Taxes (sales tax plus excise tax)

Gross domestic product is only one of several measurements of the macro economy. Here are some of the most commonly-used measurements:

Gross Domestic Product (GDP) = consumption (C) + investment (I) + government spending (G) + net exports (NX, or (X-M), or X)

Gross National Product (GNP) = GDP + receipts of factor income from the rest of the world - payments of factor income to the rest of the world

Net Domestic Product (NDP) = GDP - capital consumption allowance (depreciation)

Net national product (NNP) = GNP - capital consumption allowance (depreciation)

National income (NI) = NNP - indirect business taxes

Personal Income (PI) = NI - income earned but not received (retained corporate profits, or retained earnings; corporate income taxes, and social security contributions by firms) + income received but not earned (government transfer payments)

Disposable Income (DI) or disposable personal income (DPI) = PI - personal income taxes

Per Capita Measurements:

Comparisons of the different economies of the world, as well as comparisons of the economy of one nation over different time frames, gain additional meaning (especially in the standard of living) if the national income measurements are reported on a per capita basis. Per capita means per person, and is determined by taking the national income measurement, and dividing by the total number of people in the population.

So what is the "best" measurement of the macro economy?

GDP is the one that is most widely used. It counts the total production within the economy, so it probably is a better measurement for many kinds of comparisons than most of the other measurements. But NDP is a better measurement to reflect growth: it doesn't count replacement of capital as "new" production. GDP is more widely used than NDP because it is easier to calculate, and easier to make comparisons between different countries that may use different accounting methods. The best measurement for determining the standard of living would be real GDP per capita, but even that is not a perfect measurement of the standard of living. This measurement can tell you the changes in wealth for an "average" person in the economy, but it will not tell you if the changes in wealth are distributed equitably. If all of the gains go to a very small segment of the economy, a tiny fraction of the population, then a per capita measurement can be very misleading. And it doesn't account for the fact that many people view a "standard of living" as including things that cannot be measured in monetary terms.

Nominal and Real Values:

One of the uses of national income accounts, such as GDP, is for the comparison of an economy's performance over time. It is a measurement of economic growth. However, just looking at the value of GDP from one period of time compared to the value of GDP from another period of time will not give a meaningful indication of economic growth. This is because a change in the value of GDP has two components: a change in total output, and a change in prices (or the overall price level). To measure growth, you would need to isolate these two components, take out the price level component, and only look at the total output component.

In order to do this, economists adjust the GDP numbers by a price index to reflect the change in the overall price levels over the relevant time frame. This means that they adjust out the price level changes, leaving only the changes in output to account for a change in GDP.

The actual raw numbers for GDP are called nominal values. The numbers for GDP after the adjustment for the change in the price level are called real values. The price index used for adjusting for the price level change relating to GDP is called a GDP deflator, or GDP price index (GDPPI). The calculation is as follows:

Real GDP = Nominal GDP divided by GDPPI

In order to have a reference point for any price index, a base year is established. For the purpose of calculations, this base year can be considered to be arbitrary (although if you have to do calculations on a given set of numbers, and at the same time you have to decide what to use as the base year, you might want to pick the year that makes your calculations the easiest. Using the beginning year under consideration is often easiest). The base year has the number 100 assigned as its price index. This means that the resulting calculations must be adjusted by a factor of 100. This simply means that the decimal point is moved over two spaces. If you know the nominal values for different years, as well as the price index used for each year, you will be able to calculate not only real GDP but also GDP growth and the rate of inflation.

You may be familiar with the concept of price indexes (or indices; my dictionary lists indexes as the preferred plural). All of them are based on the prices over time of a constant bundle of goods considered to be relevant for what the index is trying to measure. Besides the GDP deflator (GDPPI) mentioned here, other price indexes include:

Consumer Price Index (CPI): Measures the prices of a "typical" bundle of goods that an "average" household purchases. Cost of living adjustments (COLAs) for people on fixed incomes, as well as many wage rates, are tied to this measurement. This measurement is far from perfect. For one thing, the economy is not made up of only "average" households that purchase "typical" bundles of goods. Differences are especially noticeable between different demographic groups, such as age groups. In addition, price changes alone can cause changes in the actual bundles of goods that consumers purchase. This is called a substitution effect. For example, if some goods in the bundle increase in price while others decrease in price, the law of demand says that consumers will tend to buy fewer of the goods with rising prices and more of the goods with falling prices, relative to each other over time. A fixed "bundle" does not take this into consideration, overstating the price index (and the rate of inflation).

The Chained Consumer Price Index (Chained CPI or C-CPI-U) is a replacement for the CPI in an attempt to eliminate the overstatement of inflation due to the substitution effect mentioned above. This measure is controversial, and at this writing is only a proposal. While proponents claim that it is a more accurate measure than CPI due to the elimination of the substitution effect, opponents insist that CPI already understates inflation for demographic groups that collect Social Security benefits (because the "typical" bundle of goods used for CPI is different from what these demographic groups tend to spend money on), and switching to a chained CPI will compound this problem. A switch from CPI to Chained CPI will lower the COLAs for the "fixed incomes" of the elderly and disabled demographics.

Producer Price Index (PPI): Formerly known as the wholesale price index (WPI), this measures the prices received by producers. This is considered to be a leading economic indicator, because it measures price changes at an earlier stage than the CPI does. If the PPI increases, it can be expected that a CPI increase will soon follow.

The Business Cycle, Unemployment, Inflation

The most widely-used measure of the health of an economy is GDP. Real GDP, measured within an economy over time, indicates whether the economy is expanding or contracting, and by how much. When real GDP is rising, the economy is growing. A healthy economy will grow over time. An increase in real GDP per capita is an indication of a rising standard of living.

Economies do not grow at a constant rate, however. At times, economies go through periods of contraction. Changes in real GDP follow a pattern, which is called the business cycle. The business cycle varies in length of time, but the pattern is always the same, a series of stages in this order: expansion, peak, contraction, and trough.

Expansion: Also called a boom period, this is a period of economic growth.

Peak: The point where expansion ends and contraction begins.

Contraction: A period of decline in real GDP. This would be a period known as a recession.

Trough: The point where contraction ends, and the cycle starts over with another expansion.

It is worth noting that the United States has had several well-publicized recessions since the 1950s, yet has averaged about 3% annual growth during the same time period. Periods of expansion tend to be longer than periods of contraction (recession). Each business cycle is different, but recessions in the United States have lasted roughly one year on the average.

Since economic growth is desirable, special focus is on recessions and their side effects.

Definition of a recession:

Recession: A period of significant decline in total output, income, employment, and trade, usually lasting from six months to a year, and marked by widespread contractions in many sectors of the economy.

This is the official definition used in the United States. It is defined by the National Bureau of Economic Research (NBER). Many people consider a recession to be two consecutive quarters of declining real GDP, but that is not the official definition. In fact, the official definition of a recession is not based on GDP statistics at all, although as a practical matter the results would probably be the same if it were. But the NBER focuses on monthly, not quarterly, data. Because real GDP is measured only quarterly, the NBER focus is on these monthly data: employment, real personal income less transfer payments, the volume of sales of manufacturing and wholesale-retail sectors adjusted for price changes, and industrial production.

Indicators:

Indicators are variables that tend to move along with the business cycle. They are classified as leading indicators, coincident indicators, and lagging indicators. Indicators are used to identify changes in the stage of the business cycle.

Leading Indicators are economic variables that tend to change before real GDP changes. Since these are changes that occur before changes in output occur, they are used to predict future output. However, leading indicators can be very unstable. Unless they move in the same direction for several consecutive months, their usefulness for predictions is limited.

Coincident indicators are economic variables that tend to change at the same time that real GDP changes.

Lagging indicators are economic variables that tend to change after real GDP changes.

Leading indicators include: average workweek; unemployment claims; manufacturers' new orders; stock prices; new plant and equipment orders; new building permits; delivery times of goods; interest rate spread; money supply; and consumer expectations.

Coincident indicators include: payroll employment; industrial production; personal income; and manufacturing and trade sales.

Lagging indicators include: labor cost per unit of output; inventory sales ratio; unemployment duration; consumer credit to personal income ratio; outstanding commercial loans; prime interest rate; and inflation rate for services.

Unemployment:

Economists have identified four categories of unemployment: structural unemployment, frictional unemployment, cyclical unemployment, and seasonal unemployment.

Structural unemployment is the type of unemployment that is caused by job-seekers not having the skills necessary to fill the open positions. It implies that enough jobs are available in the economy for these job-seekers, but the people who make hiring decisions don't believe that the job-seekers are qualified for the positions that are available. Structural unemployment is often associated with changes in technology. New technology often requires new job skills, and jobs that require older technology are eliminated. Structural unemployment is considered to be part of the natural rate of unemployment.

Frictional unemployment is the unemployment that arises from the fact that there is always a time gap between the time when a person without a job starts actively looking for a job, and the time when that person finds a job. In a dynamic economy, many people will fall into this category at any point in time, including the time when the unemployment statistics are compiled. Frictional unemployment is considered to be part of the natural rate of unemployment.

Cyclical unemployment is the unemployment that is associated with an economy that is operating at below its full-employment, or optimal, level of output. Cyclical unemployment is directly caused by a downturn in the business cycle. It is most closely associated with a recession. Since it is caused by a down economy, cyclical unemployment is not part of the natural rate of unemployment.

Seasonal unemployment is the unemployment caused by the fact that some jobs have busy seasons and slow seasons. During the slow seasons, many workers are laid off, but will be expected to be rehired once the busy season returns. Seasonal unemployment is considered to be part of the natural rate of unemployment.

Calculating the Unemployment Rate:

The unemployment rate is equal to the number of people classified as unemployed divided by the total labor force, expressed as a percentage.

This formula requires definitions of relevant terms:

Unemployed persons: Only people without jobs who are actively looking for work are counted as being unemployed. This means that discouraged workers, and others not active in a job search, are not counted. The U.S. Department of Labor considers a person to be actively looking for work if that person is available for work and has looked for work within the past four weeks; or is waiting for a recall after being laid off; or is starting a job within 30 days.

Total labor force is defined as the number of employed persons plus the number of persons counted as unemployed. This means that people with jobs are counted as employed, even though many of them may be considered underemployed (for example, they may be working part time but are looking for full time work). The formula used by the U.S. Department of Labor excludes the following residents from the total labor force: residents under 16 years of age, institutionalized adults, and adults not looking for work.

Other terms associated with a discussion of unemployment, even though they are not part of the unemployment rate calculations:

Discouraged workers: Discouraged workers are people without jobs who have given up looking for work, and are no longer active in their job searches. These people are not counted as being part of the total labor force, and are not counted as unemployed. They are not part of the unemployment statistics.

Total population: This is the number of people who live in the economy, including those who are too young to be counted as part of the labor force and those who are retired.

Working age population: The total population minus the people who are either too young or too old to be considered part of the labor force.

Labor force participation rate: The percentage of the working age population that is counted in the total labor force. This includes those who are counted as employed as well as those who are counted as unemployed.

In the United States, the official unemployment statistics are compiled and published on a monthly basis by the Bureau of Labor Statistics, which is a division of the Department of Labor.

The Bureau of Labor Statistics compiles these statistics by taking an extensive survey of U.S. households. It is this survey that determines the official unemployment rate and other statistics each month. Some people mistakenly believe that the unemployment rate is based on the number of claims for jobless benefits. Those numbers are compiled weekly, not monthly, and have nothing to do with the unemployment statistics.

The following example is based on a hypothetical country using this data:

Total population: 100,000,000

Working age population: 75,000,000

Residents employed full-time: 40,000,000

Residents employed part-time: 15,000,000

Non-employed adults actively seeking employment: 5,000,000

Discouraged workers: 1,000,000

In this example, the number of employed persons is 55,000,000. For calculating labor statistics, it doesn't matter whether a person is employed full time or part time.

The number of unemployed persons is 5,000,000. Only those residents who are not employed and also are actively seeking work are counted as unemployed.

The total labor force is 60,000,000. This is the sum of those counted as employed and those counted as unemployed.

The labor force participation rate is 80%. This is the percentage of the working age population that is counted in the total labor force. In this example, that would be 60,000,000 divided by 75,000,000.

The unemployment rate is 8.33%. This is the percentage of the total labor force that is counted as unemployed. In this example, that would be 5,000,000 divided by 60,000,000.

How reliable are the official unemployment statistics? The survey conducted by the Bureau of Labor Statistics is extensive enough to be considered statistically significant, so the numbers should be reliable. But they ignore two important categories of citizens: the hidden unemployed and the hidden employed.

The hidden unemployed are mentioned above. They include discouraged workers and underemployed workers. Discouraged workers are actually unemployed workers who have given up their job search. They want to work, but they have determined that nobody will hire them, so they have quit actively seeking work. They are considered to be those who have looked for work in the past year, but not within the past four weeks. Underemployed workers are those who have jobs but are not using all of their productive potential. They are counted as employed, but they would prefer to be doing something more productive. This includes part time workers who would prefer to be working full time, and full time workers who have jobs that do not utilize their particular job skills.

The hidden employed would be workers in the underground economy. These are people with jobs and incomes that go unreported. As a result of not reporting their jobs, they may be counted as unemployed. These jobs are unreported for a variety of reasons. They represent unreported taxable income. Self-employment or employer / employee taxes are being avoided. Jobs may be unreported in order to avoid minimum wage laws or other regulations or reporting requirements. Income earned as a result of illegal activity is almost always unreported. Jobs may be unreported in order to avoid immigration laws. The size of the underground economy is often blamed entirely on illegal immigration; but while it is clear that many people in the underground economy are illegal immigrants, many others are not. It is not clear, however, what the overall size of the underground economy is.

The effect of minimum wage laws on unemployment:

Think back to the discussion of supply and demand, especially in reference to the labor market. In the market for labor, a legal minimum wage is a price floor. The price in the labor market is the wage rate. An effective price floor would be set above the equilibrium price. This means that the supply of labor would be higher than the demand for labor at that price (wage rate). A surplus is the result. More people would be willing and able to work at that wage rate than businesses would be willing to hire at that wage rate. The number of workers hired would be lower than the number of workers who would have been hired at the equilibrium price in the absence of a minimum wage law. Fewer people will be employed and more people will be classified as unemployed. More people are out of work as a result.

It is important to note which groups of people will be affected by minimum wage laws. Minimum wage laws increase the cost of production. This means a decrease in the supply of goods and services, resulting in higher prices and lower quantities available for consumers.

Minimum wage laws do not just affect the wages of workers who work for minimum wage. If employers are forced to pay higher wages to their least productive and most inexperienced workers, they are also likely to raise the pay for more productive workers. This will allow them to provide an incentive to their workers to become more efficient. This also will mean higher production costs and the resulting decrease in supply. This will magnify the amount of the labor surplus, creating more unemployment.

Many small businesses and start-up companies are especially affected by minimum wage laws. These are the kinds of businesses that are most likely to depend on low labor costs in order to survive. One of the costs to society of minimum wage laws is the amount of economic growth that does not occur because of higher input prices preventing an increase in supply. Since small businesses tend to be the largest source of new jobs, this creates a permanently higher unemployment rate and a decrease in output.

Perhaps the largest cost of minimum wage laws is one that cannot accurately be measured: the number of potential businesses that do not even get started because of higher labor costs. Probably many people have ideas for starting a business, but the ideas never materialize because the labor costs make them unfeasible. New businesses often need time to produce an economically viable revenue stream. As a result, the mobility of people moving into the entrepreneur class is curtailed.

With all of the costs associated with minimum wage laws, why do they even exist at all? One obvious answer is that politicians can appear to be doing something for the working class. But besides this feel-good reason, there are real benefits associated with minimum wage laws.

Many people rely on jobs that pay minimum wage for their living standards. These jobs are the only source of income for many people. It is not true, as many people assert, that minimum wage jobs only go to teenagers working part time, or that minimum wage jobs only represent short term situations for people who will be earning higher wages very soon. For many people, especially in rural areas, minimum wage jobs are the only available options for working careers. For the people who have these jobs, the minimum wage laws may prevent poverty. Minimum wage laws decrease the costs of welfare programs provided by the government. To the extent that minimum wages reduce public assistance to low-income individuals, they represent a cost shift from taxpayers to employers who hire workers at low wages.

Minimum wage laws have been developed largely as a result of market failure. Historical evidence points to workers being exploited by employers in the absence of government intervention. This kind of market failure means that workers are not always compensated for their contributions, for their increased productivity, as economic theory would suggest. Much historical evidence suggests that employers will be able to exploit workers if they are legally allowed to do so. When this happens, the minimum wage laws may be the only way to keep a large percentage of the labor force from working at wages that are below poverty level. This point of view means that minimum wage laws are a source of correcting for existing market failure, enhancing rather than decreasing the power of markets to create efficient results.

112

The amount of unemployment and its associated costs resulting from minimum wage laws may be greatly overstated. It depends on the elasticity of demand and the elasticity of supply. With the labor demand lower than the labor supply at the wage rate of an effective minimum wage, the difference between labor demand and labor supply would be the amount of an increase in unemployment due to the minimum wage law, according to the definitions of unemployment and the method used to compile unemployment statistics. However, this does not mean that the entire increase in unemployment is due to workers who would have had jobs in the absence of a minimum wage law. Only the amount by which the number of workers hired is below the free market equilibrium quantity, not the total below the labor supply curve, represents people who have lost jobs due to the minimum wage. The rest of the difference between supply and demand, which would be the difference between the market equilibrium quantity and the labor supply quantity at the minimum wage, represents people who would not have had jobs anyway. They would not have looked for work at the equilibrium rate, but they would look for work at the minimum wage rate. They simply get reclassified from not in the labor force to unemployed when they begin to look for work. How much of the unemployment represents people who would have had jobs at the equilibrium rate, and how much simply represents people who are reclassified but wouldn't have jobs in either case, depends on the elasticity of supply and demand in the labor market.

To understand the concept that minimum wages only create unemployment in some cases, consider the kinds of businesses that are affected by minimum wage laws. The above analysis of the costs associated with minimum wage laws was based on some generic firm. The picture looks different if you consider specific kinds of businesses, and the options that they have for responding to increased labor costs due to minimum wage laws.

Businesses that face an increase in costs due to an increase in the minimum wage can respond by using one or some combination of the following:

They can decide that they cannot afford to stay in business, and shut down.

They can increase their prices, passing the additional costs on to their customers.

They can reduce the number of work hours that they hire, which involves decreasing production or increasing efficiency.

They can move production to another country with lower labor costs.

They can simply pay the extra labor costs by reducing profits.

Now, consider the types of businesses that tend to employ minimum wage workers in a given geographic area. You may be able to get a general idea of which of the above options these businesses are likely to utilize, and what the actual costs of an increase in the minimum wage are in that geographic area.

The costs of unemployment:

Unemployment has many negative consequences for society. Some of the important ones are a GDP output gap; a distribution effect; and social costs.

GDP output gap:

When unemployment increases, the nation's total output falls below potential output, reducing the standard of living. Potential GDP is the level of GDP when unemployment is at the natural rate of unemployment. When unemployment is higher than the natural rate, it creates a shortfall of GDP below potential GDP. This shortfall is called the output gap.

The natural rate of unemployment is called the non-accelerating inflation rate of unemployment (NAIRU). This is the lowest unemployment rate consistent with not putting upward pressure on prices and wages.

You may be accustomed to the term "full employment" instead of "natural rate of unemployment". Your class or textbook may even use that term. Many economists are moving away from using the term "full employment" because it has caused confusion. Full employment does not mean zero unemployment. Frictional, structural, and seasonal unemployment always exist in a dynamic economy. "Natural rate of unemployment" implies a realistic level of output.

Measuring the natural rate of unemployment is difficult. It changes over time, and the GDP gap at any given time is difficult to measure. It is different in different countries with different policies and labor markets. Economists tend to agree that in the United States, the natural rate of unemployment varies over time between 4% and 7%.

Business investment falls during times of high unemployment, which could cause the future level of output to decrease as well.

How large is the GDP output gap for a given level of unemployment? One rule of thumb to measure the output gap is called Okun's Law. Okun's Law states that for every 1% that the unemployment rate increases above the natural rate of unemployment, the output gap increases by 2.5%. Okun's Law is quantified using this formula:

((Potential GDP minus actual GDP) divided by actual GDP) x 100 = (actual unemployment rate minus the natural unemployment rate).

Distribution Effect:

A high rate of unemployment does not affect everybody equally. Its negative impact is felt mostly by the unemployed persons themselves, and their families. These are the persons who suffer from a loss of income, a lower standard of living, and a loss of social status. Moreover, high unemployment tends to impact disadvantaged demographic groups more than others. Young workers, unskilled workers, and minority groups tend to have higher rates of unemployment than other groups.

Unemployment tends to redistribute wealth from the lower classes to the upper classes.

Social Costs:

High unemployment is associated with such social costs as high crime rates and alcoholism. Infrastructure and public services suffer due to lower tax revenues. Lower investments in education, combined with the negative effect of unemployment on the motivation of young people, can impact all of the costs associated with unemployment for future generations.

Inflation:

You do not need to possess a degree in economics in order to understand many of the effects of inflation. Almost everybody has had to learn to deal with the consequences of inflation at some point in their lives. But misconceptions still exist. It would be helpful to know what the inflation rate means, as well as possible causes and solutions.

The definition of inflation would be a good starting point:

Inflation: A sustained rise in the average level of prices.

Not all prices change at the same time or by the same amount. The inflation rate measures average, not individual, price changes.

Inflation represents a decline in the purchasing power of the currency. As prices rise, the same nominal value of the currency will be worth less in terms of the amount of goods and services that it can be used to purchase. An alternative definition of inflation would be:

Inflation: A sustained decline in the value of the currency.

Price Indexes:

It would be impossible to track the price changes and quantities sold for every good and service in a complex economy. Besides, different price indexes are used to measure the degree that inflation affects different groups of people. Therefore, only prices and quantities for something considered to be a "typical" bundle of goods are included in the calculations. The inflation rate measures average price changes over time. This is done by assigning a number, called a price index, to the average price level for each time period (usually one year). A change in the price index from one year to another would indicate the level of inflation.

Common price indexes in use in the United States include the GDP Deflator (also known as the GDP Price Index, or GDPPI), the Consumer Price Index (CPI), and the Producer Price Index (PPI).

Interest rates and inflation:

What are interest rates?

When a borrower (debtor) and a lender (creditor) enter into a contract, the borrower receives funds at the present time from the lender in exchange for paying the funds back at a later time. In essence, the borrower has gained control of the use of money that is owned by the lender. This includes the opportunity to invest this money for the purpose of earning income for the borrower.

The lender is willing to enter into such a contract because income for the lender is involved. The borrower agrees to pay back money in addition to the amount of money borrowed in order to compensate the lender for providing this service. The amount of funds borrowed is called principle. The amount in addition to the principle that the borrower agrees to pay to compensate the lender is called interest.

The amount of the interest, stated as a percentage of the principle and annualized, is called the interest rate. This concept is known as the time value of money.

To the borrower, interest represents a cost of borrowing, called interest expense. To the lender, interest represents income on an investment, since the lender is investing funds in the transaction in order to earn income. This is called interest income.

This analysis applies to the bond market as well as such transactions as bank loans, because bonds are actually contracts between lenders and borrowers.

At any given time, different rates of interest will be present for different transactions and different types of transactions. This is because any given interest rate will have at least four different components, which can vary from transaction to transaction (and from situation to situation):

The time value of money: this is the rate of interest that would induce a lender to enter into a transaction in a risk-free environment. This amount would vary with the state of the economy, but would be theoretical in nature, since risk is always involved. It would be equal to the opportunity cost of the transaction.

Risk premium: this is the portion of the interest rate in addition to the time value of money associated with the risk of default.

Liquidity and marketability: All else equal, a loan that is liquid and marketable would be preferable to a loan that is less liquid or less marketable. A higher interest rate on the less liquid and less marketable loan would compensate for this difference.

Anticipated inflation: The portion of the interest rate designed to compensate the lender for the decrease in purchasing power due to inflation during the time that the loan proceeds are outstanding.

This is explained in more detail below.

The effects of inflation on interest rates:

When inflation is present, the borrower receives money that is worth more than the money that is paid back. In order for such a transaction to take place, both the borrower and the lender will have to agree on the terms. This can occur as long as the effects of inflation are built into the contract.

When the inflation rate is included as part of the stated interest rate, the lender will be compensated for the loss of purchasing power during the time that the loan is outstanding, or during the time that control over the money is transferred from the lender to the borrower. By including the inflation rate in the stated interest rate, the contract can be mutually acceptable to both the borrower and the lender, despite the loss of purchasing power over time.

The stated interest rate, which includes the adjustment for inflation, is called the nominal interest rate. The effective interest rate, after the effects of inflation are discounted, is called the real interest rate.

The formula for this is:

118

Real interest rate = nominal interest rate minus inflation rate

Including the inflation rate in the nominal interest rate will mean that neither the borrower nor the lender can gain a windfall profit at the other's expense simply because of inflation.

The problem with that concept is that the contract involves payments to be made in the future. In order to include the inflation rate in the nominal interest rate, the future inflation rate must be known. Since it is impossible to know with certainty what the future inflation rate will be, the rate of inflation must be forecast. This is accomplished using the concept of expected, or anticipated, inflation.

The anticipated inflation rate is the expected rate of inflation over the length of the contract. As long as the actual inflation rate turns out to be equal to the anticipated inflation rate, inflation will not redistribute wealth between the parties to the contract. Each party will receive a perceived benefit from the transaction.

However, when the actual inflation rate differs from the anticipated inflation rate, wealth is redistributed between the parties simply because of the existence of inflation.

When the actual rate of inflation is greater than the anticipated rate of inflation, the borrower ends up paying back the loan with money that is worth less than contracted for. In that case, the borrower gains at the expense of the lender. In the aggregate, wealth is redistributed from the creditor class to the debtor class.

When the actual rate of inflation is less than the anticipated rate of inflation, the opposite occurs. The borrower ends up paying back the loan with money that is worth more than contracted for. In that case, the lender gains at the expense of the borrower. In the aggregate, wealth is redistributed from the debtor class to the creditor class.

It should be worth noting that this analysis holds for all contracts involving interest rates. This means that the debtor class includes households with outstanding personal loans, homeowners with outstanding mortgages, corporations with outstanding bonds, and governments with outstanding bonds. The creditor class includes banks and other financial institutions, as well as investors in corporate and government bonds.

In the case of government debt, for example, when the actual rate of inflation is greater than the anticipated rate of inflation, wealth is redistributed from the investor class to the taxpayer class. When the actual rate of inflation is less than the anticipated rate of inflation, wealth is redistributed from the taxpayer class to the investor class. And in the case of foreign ownership of bonds, wealth can be transferred from one country to another.

In addition to the redistribution effect of interest rates explained above, the consequences of inflation include redistribution due to sticky prices, uncertainty and inefficient resource allocation.

Inflation causes redistribution to occur when specific wages and prices do not adjust with the rate of inflation, such as pension payments of retirees that are fixed at a specific level. The term "fixed income" refers to this situation. Those who receive such payments will face a decrease in purchasing power during times of inflation. The effects of redistribution can be minimized if wages and prices are indexed for inflation. That is, if the payments are adjusted based on changes in a relevant price index.

Inflation creates uncertainty regarding the future profitability of investments. This is especially true during times when the inflation rate is high. High inflation rates tend to be volatile. This can cause risk aversion to investments that could otherwise create future economic growth. Funds get reallocated from long term to short term projects. Funds also get reallocated from interest-sensitive investments, ones that could produce economic growth, to inflation hedges such as gold and real estate. As a result, long term economic growth is decreased.

Inflation can also result in inefficient resource allocation. Long term contracts become riskier in times of high inflation. The market for long term bonds is decreased in favor of short term investments. Labor contracts and wage scales are set for shorter periods. Holding money becomes risky, because money balances depreciate in value. All of this requires that more time be spent on financial transactions, making less time available for productive activities. The costs associated with this inefficient resource allocation are called the shoe-leather costs of inflation.

Inflation can be caused by forces that work on aggregate demand, called demand-pull inflation; or by forces that work on aggregate supply, called cost-push inflation.

Demand-Pull Inflation:

The aggregate demand and aggregate supply model shows that the price level increases whenever aggregate demand increases (when the AD curve shifts rightward). This can be a permanent situation due to continual increases in the money supply and government spending. Wars generally create demand-pull inflation because of government borrowing to finance war efforts.

Cost-Push Inflation:

The aggregate demand and aggregate supply model shows that the price level increases whenever aggregate supply decreases (when the AS curve shifts leftward). This is not a permanent situation, because the general trend is for aggregate supply to shift rightward. Occasionally it can shift leftward due to a supply shock: a sudden decrease in aggregate supply. Examples are weather related reductions in the production of basic foods, large cutbacks in oil production, and a large increase in the minimum wage.

A supply shock results in both higher prices and lower output. In this case, both high inflation and high unemployment can occur at the same time. This is called stagflation, and occurred in many industrialized nations during the 1970s.

The Money Supply and Inflation:

Perhaps you have heard people say that inflation is always caused by an over-supply of money, created by government action. Perhaps you already believe that to be true. Many people do. In that case, the above explanations for the causes of inflation can be interpreted in terms of the underlying supply of money.

However, consider the following situation:

Suppose that the world supply of oil was suddenly reduced drastically, as it was in the 1970s. This would be a classic case of supply shock. The aggregate supply curve shifts leftward, resulting in both higher inflation and higher unemployment.

Now also suppose that the government decides to intervene with stimulus monetary and/or fiscal policies in order to reduce unemployment. In this case, the government believes that the best short run policy would be to stimulate output and employment. Expansionary government policy to deal with the situation will shift the aggregate demand curve to the right.

This will create more output and lower unemployment, but will also magnify the inflation problem. So, how does the situation coincide with the belief that inflation is always caused by an increase in the underlying money supply? After all, the initial inflationary pressures had nothing to do with the money supply, but the government response did.

Some people will look at the government's reaction first, and say that the money supply caused this inflation. Most economists would not agree with that assessment.

The relationship between inflation and unemployment:

The Phillips Curve is a graph that illustrates the observed relationship between the inflation rate and the unemployment rate. It is a downward sloping curve, indicating that a trade-off exists between inflation and unemployment.

This has important implications for government policies that attempt to achieve economic stability. Expansionary policies may reduce unemployment at the expense of higher inflation. Contractionary policies may reduce inflation at the cost of higher unemployment. Activist government policies, then, require that the costs and benefits associated with such policies be considered. Policies tend to adjust as economic realities change the perceived costs and benefits over time.

Why does the relationship between inflation and unemployment exist? Economists have come up with a few possible reasons: leverage on wages; production bottlenecks; and normal shifts in aggregate demand and aggregate supply.

Leverage on Wages:

Changes in the price level are closely related to changes in wage rates. In fact, the original Phillips Curve was developed to show the observed relationship between wage inflation, not price inflation, and unemployment. Economists at a later time changed it to show price inflation in part because of an observed close relationship between wage inflation and price inflation. Wages contribute a large share of the costs of production.

During times of economic expansion, profits are high and few replacement workers are available. Workers are in a good position to bargain for higher wages. Businesses would stand to lose a lot of profits if a labor strike occurred. With aggregate demand high, businesses can more easily pass along the increase in labor costs to their customers in the form of higher prices. The result of this situation: Low unemployment resulting in upward pressure on wages and prices. Unemployment decreases while inflation increases.

However, when unemployment is high, businesses have more leverage than workers. Workers can be more easily replaced because of the large pool of unemployed workers. Sales and profits are low, so the opportunity costs of a strike will be relatively low. Workers know the possibility of unemployment is very real, and the priority of keeping a job increases relative to the priority of wage increases. The result of the situation of high unemployment is little upward pressure on wages and prices. Unemployment increases while inflation decreases.

Production Bottlenecks:

When output is low and unemployment is high, excess capacity exists. The economy will have little incentive for price increases. But when aggregate demand increases, output increases and unemployment decreases. Excess capacity decreases. As businesses reach capacity, they reach a limit of how much they can produce in the short run. As a result of increased demand and production limits, prices will increase. The result of this situation: unemployment decreases while inflation increases.

Normal Shifts in Aggregate Demand and Aggregate Supply:

The Aggregate Demand and Aggregate Supply model is a graph that plots a nation's price level against the level of real output. In this model, an increase in the price level would be equivalent to inflation. A decrease in output could be considered a substitute for unemployment, since unemployment tends to increase when output decreases.

This trade-off between inflation and unemployment would be associated with a shift in aggregate demand, since the aggregate demand curve is downward sloping. The aggregate supply curve is upward sloping: a shift in aggregate supply would not indicate a trade-off between inflation and unemployment. Inflation and unemployment both increase when the aggregate supply curve shifts leftward. This situation is called stagflation, usually caused by a supply shock.

Economic forces cause the aggregate demand and aggregate supply curves to shift constantly. The general trend over time, however, is for both curves to shift rightward. Aggregate demand shifts rightward as the money supply increases, and as household and government spending increase. Aggregate supply shifts rightward as resources (labor and capital) are increased, and as technology increases.

The normal trend is for aggregate demand to shift more than aggregate supply. When that happens, given that both curves tend to shift rightward, over time the new equilibrium created with each shift will show that prices increase when output increases. Since an output increase generally reflects a decrease in unemployment, this would create a normal trend that mirrors a trade-off between inflation and unemployment.

Many economists believe that in the long run, the actual unemployment rate will equal the natural rate of unemployment. In this case, the long run Phillips Curve is a vertical line at the natural rate of unemployment. According to this theory, no trade-off exists between inflation and unemployment in the long run.

Hyperinflation:

Hyperinflation is a situation in which the rate of inflation accelerates to the point where the entire economy breaks down.

Nobody wants to receive currency in exchange for goods and services because the currency will soon lose its value. It will be worth less than the value of the goods and services that it was exchanged for. In an attempt to prevent that from happening, people will rush to spend the money before it loses its value. This increases current demand, drastically decreases long term investments, and makes the hyperinflation situation worse.

Hyperinflation, despite being talked about a lot, has actually occurred relatively infrequently in recorded world history. In each case, it has happened during times of political instability, and was created by unstable governments printing a very large quantity of money instead of collecting taxes. Typically in these situations, the government is either unwilling or unable to collect taxes to prevent hyperinflation from occurring.

The usual response to hyperinflation is for the currency to be replaced by a new currency. Often, because of the unstable situation, the government is also replaced. The chances of hyperinflation occurring without a civil war or an overthrow of the government contributing to the causes of hyperinflation are remotely small in the industrialized world.

Is there a specific rate of inflation that defines hyperinflation? I have not seen a number that economists tend to agree with, but it would be very high. The number that I have seen quoted most often is an inflation rate of 50% per month, or higher. But I don't believe that the economics profession has defined hyperinflation with a specific number.

Deflation:

Deflation is defined as a period of time in which the price level decreases. Alternatively, it can be defined as a period of time in which the value of the currency rises.

During periods of deflation, businesses may have difficulty making payments on their investment obligations. They sell goods and services at deflated prices, but have to make principle and interest payments based on pre-deflated values of the currency. Real interest rates are higher than nominal interest rates. As a result, businesses and farms are more likely to become bankrupt.

Aggregate Demand and Aggregate Supply

The aggregate demand (AD) curve and the aggregate supply (AS) curve are used in macroeconomics to help explain changes in the overall condition of an economy. The AD/AS model is a graph that explains the concepts behind the causes of changes in real GDP and the overall level of prices. This tool helps explain the business cycle, cyclical unemployment, and inflation. This tool is similar to supply and demand in microeconomics in the sense that it involves a downward sloping aggregate demand curve similar to a downward sloping demand curve, and an upward sloping aggregate supply curve similar to an upward sloping supply curve.

The determinants of aggregate demand and aggregate supply are different from the determinants of demand and supply in microeconomics, but the two models are related. For example, the sum of all demand curves in an economy would comprise a large portion of the aggregate demand curve.

Microeconomic changes that only relate to individual demand and supply curves are not considered to be large enough to create changes in the AD/AS model unless these changes have implications throughout the entire economy.

The aggregate demand and aggregate supply model is a graph that plots the overall price level on the vertical axis and real GDP on the horizontal axis. Changes depicted by this model reflect economic growth as well as the rate of inflation and the unemployment rate. Changes in real GDP represent changes in output, which is economic growth. The unemployment rate is closely tied to changes in output: when output increases, employment tends to increase and unemployment tends to decrease. A negative correlation exists between output and the unemployment rate. The rate of inflation can be considered to be equal to changes in the price level.

Aggregate demand is the total of all expenditures in the economy. Total expenditures in the AD/AS model equal real GDP. Using the expenditures approach, GDP equals the sum of consumption (household sector), investment (business sector), government purchases (government sector), and net exports (international sector). The factors of aggregate demand are the factors that influence spending by each of these sectors:

Household sector: the factors of household consumption are income, wealth, expectations, demographics, and taxes.

Income: an increase in income will increase consumption.

Wealth: an increase in wealth will increase consumption.

Expectations: consumer confidence influences consumption. If consumers are confident that income and wealth will increase in the future, current consumption will rise. If consumers fear a job loss or a recession, current consumption will fall.

Demographics: total population and age distribution affect consumption. An increase in the total population will increase consumption. Older and younger households tend to spend more and save less (have a higher MPC) than households in the middle of the age groups.

Taxes: the amount of taxes helps determine the level of disposable income, and therefore influences the amount of consumption spending.

Business sector: the level of business investment depends on the profitability of investments, which depends on interest rates, technology, the cost of capital goods, and excess capacity.

Interest rates: a large portion of investment is financed through borrowing. Interest is the cost of borrowing. The level of investment is inversely related to the interest rate.

Technology: new technology increases investment. Firms change to new methods in order to remain competitive.

The cost of capital goods: an increase in the cost of production reduces profits. Lower profit potential will reduce investment spending.

Excess capacity: output can be increased without new investment if excess capacity exists. More excess capacity in the economy means a lower level of investment spending.

Government sector: government purchases increase aggregate demand by the amount of the purchases. In addition, government purchases add money to the economy which is then subject to a multiplier effect. The multiplier effect for government purchases is greater than the multiplier effect for household income, since households have an MPC that is less than one (they will save a portion of income instead of spending all of it). The money that the government adds to the economy through government purchases may increase the price level. The level of government spending is often the result of discretionary fiscal policy.

International sector: exports increase aggregate demand while imports decrease aggregate demand. The level of exports depends on factors in the rest of the world. The level of imports is determined by domestic factors. These factors are income, prices, exchange rates, and government policy.

Income: a portion of consumption will be for goods from the rest of the world. When foreign incomes rise, exports increase. When domestic incomes rise, imports increase.

Prices: when the prices of domestic goods change relative to the prices of foreign goods, net exports will change. Higher domestic prices will increase imports. Higher foreign prices will increase exports.

Exchange rates: when the domestic currency depreciates on the foreign exchange market, domestic goods become cheaper to foreign buyers and exports will increase. Imports will decrease at the same time because the change in the exchange rate will make foreign goods more expensive for domestic buyers.

Government policy: trade restrictions imposed by governments limit the amount of exports and/or imports.

These factors of aggregate demand include both price factors and non-price factors. Changes in the price factors will cause a cause a movement along the AD curve. Changes in the non-price factors will cause a shift in the entire AD curve. This distinction is due to the fact that the price level is plotted along the vertical axis.

Price factors of aggregate demand are divided into three categories: the wealth effect, the interest rate effect, and the international trade effect. A change in any of these categories will cause a movement along the AD curve.

Wealth effect: financial assets (money, stocks, and bonds) represent purchasing power. This purchasing power changes inversely with changes in the price level. For any given nominal value of financial assets, a higher the price level will result in a lower purchasing power, and therefore lower real wealth.

Interest rate effect: as the price level increases, more money is needed for purchases. This increases the demand for money, and lowers the demand for other financial assets such as bonds. A lower demand for bonds will decrease the price of bonds, increasing interest rates. Higher interest rates will create a decrease in aggregate investment spending.

International trade effect: changes in the relative prices of foreign and domestic goods will cause changes in net exports. These are changes in the overall price level, creating a movement along the AD curve.

These price factors of aggregate demand give the AD curve its downward slope.

The price factors of aggregate demand (wealth effect, interest rate effect, and international trade effect) show different real GDP levels at different price levels. Changes in all of the factors that affect consumption, investment, government purchases, and net exports can also cause real GDP to change at every price level. All factors of aggregate demand, whether or not they are price factors, are also non-price factors. Changes in the non-price factors of aggregate demand will cause the entire AD curve to shift.

The aggregate supply (AS) curve is a graph of the level of real GDP that firms will be willing to produce at various price levels. The aggregate supply curve is different in the short run than in the long run.

Firms are willing to supply more output whenever profitability increases. An increase in the prices of output, holding all other factors constant, will increase profitability and the level of real output. This means that a positive relationship exists between the price level and the real GDP supplied. The AS curve slopes upward.

The aggregate supply curve becomes steeper as the price level rises. This is because at higher levels of output, more firms reach capacity and cannot respond to higher prices with an increase in output, at least in the short run.

The upward slope of the AS curve generally holds true in the short run. Holding all other factors constant is at least partially realistic in the short run. Profits increase with a higher price level in the short run because input prices tend to be more inflexible than output prices. For example, wage rates may be set by contract and are based on historical or expected price levels, not actual price levels. A time lag may also exist before suppliers raise their prices.

In the long run, however, input prices have time to adjust to changes in the price level. Real profits will not necessarily increase with a higher price level. With no increase in long run profits, the aggregate supply curve loses its upward slope. As a result, in the long run real GDP will not change with a price level change. The long run aggregate supply curve becomes a vertical line.

Many economists agree that this vertical line is at the level of real GDP that coincides with the natural rate of unemployment. This means that long run real GDP would be equal to potential GDP.

This vertical long run aggregate supply curve, at the natural rate of unemployment level of output, does not mean that long run real GDP is fixed. Both the long run and the short run aggregate supply curves shift as changes occur in the non-price determinants of aggregate supply. Technological advances and increases in resources allow for economic growth in the long run.

The non-price determinants of aggregate supply are resource prices, technology, and expectations.

Resource prices: as stated above, resource prices do not fully adjust to changes in the overall price level in the short run. When resource prices do change, profitability and the level of aggregate supply also change. An increase in resource prices will shift the AS curve to the left. Only changes in the prices of resources, and not changes in the overall price level, will create this shift in the aggregate supply curve.

Technology: technological advances increase efficiency. New technology allows more output to be produced with the same level of resource inputs. This lowers the costs of production. As a result, firms are willing to supply more output, and the AS curve shifts to the right.

Expectations: expectations of the future price level will cause shifts in the current aggregate supply curve. When wage contracts are renewed, an expected increase in the price level can cause an increase in current input prices, reducing aggregate supply. Expectations of higher prices shift the AS curve to the left. Since a leftward shift in the aggregate supply curve creates a higher price level, this means that anticipated higher prices can cause higher prices. In effect, the expectation of inflation becomes a self-fulfilling prophesy.

Equilibrium in the aggregate demand and aggregate supply model:

The aggregate demand curve slopes downward. The short run aggregate supply curve slopes upward. The point where these two curves intersect indicates the short run equilibrium price level and real GDP.

If this is also long run equilibrium, then it would indicate a level of real GDP that is equal to potential GDP. The long run aggregate supply curve would be a vertical line that runs through this point.

What happens to the equilibrium price level and equilibrium real GDP when changes in the economy cause the positions of these curves to shift?

Consider two scenarios: first, one in which a change in the economy is created by a change in aggregate demand; second, one in which a change in the economy is created by a change in aggregate supply. These scenarios assume an initial position of short run and long run equilibrium.

Scenario 1: Shift in aggregate demand:

If aggregate demand increases due to changes in any of the non-price determinants of aggregate demand, the aggregate demand curve shifts to the right. This intersects the short run aggregate supply curve at a different point, creating a new short run equilibrium situation with a higher price level and a higher real GDP than the original equilibrium.

In this case, the equilibrium real GDP will be above potential GDP. But this is not long run equilibrium. This point is away from the long run aggregate supply curve. In the long run, as input prices adjust to the new (higher) price level, the short run aggregate supply curve will shift leftward, until it intersects the new aggregate demand curve along the long run aggregate supply curve.

At this point, the initial increase in real GDP has not been sustained. The new long run equilibrium is at the original level of real GDP. The only change in long run equilibrium is a higher price level. This higher price level represents inflation. Since the initial cause of the change in equilibrium is an increase in aggregate demand, this type of inflation is called demand-pull inflation.

Scenario 2: Shift in aggregate supply:

If the initial change in equilibrium is a sudden increase in the price of a key input, the short run aggregate supply curve shifts to the left. This intersects the aggregate demand curve at a different point, creating a new equilibrium with a higher price level and a lower real GDP than the original equilibrium. In this case, the result is higher prices and lower output, a situation called stagflation. The type of inflation caused by a decrease in aggregate supply is called cost-push inflation. Stagflation caused by a sudden leftward shift in the aggregate supply curve is called supply shock.

This leftward shift in the aggregate supply curve may or may not be permanent. It is unlikely that such a supply shock will continue to push the aggregate supply curve further to the left. Events that create supply shock tend to be independent, one-time events. If the initial cause of the supply shock is a weather event or a natural

132

disaster, the aggregate supply curve will eventually shift back to the original equilibrium position.

If the cause of the supply shock is man-made, such as a decision by oil producers to decrease global supplies, the shift in the short run aggregate supply curve could shift the long run aggregate supply curve to the left as well. This would mean that the price level increase could be permanent, long run equilibrium real GDP could be lower, and the natural rate of unemployment could increase.

Paradox of Thrift

The paradox of thrift is also known as the paradox of saving.

The paradox of thrift states that during a recession, an increase in planned savings (in other words, when the marginal propensity to save increases) can cause actual savings and investment to decrease. The plan is to save more, but the macro result of the plan is the opposite of the plan. This can prolong or deepen a recession.

It is not unusual for people to reduce consumption spending in recessionary times. Obviously, those who have lost disposable income due to the recession will have less money to spend. But others will often reduce consumption also, as a hedge against the increased possibility of a future loss of income.

Since consumption plus savings equals disposable income, and the marginal propensity to consume (MPC) plus the marginal propensity to save (MPS) always equals one by mathematical definition, then a decrease in consumption at a given level of disposable income will mean that savings will increase. The paradox of thrift is a theory that says that in such a situation, the level of disposable income will not stay the same. In fact, the increase in the MPS will cause the level of disposable income to decrease.

This means that the expected increase in savings from the increase in the MPS will not occur. In fact, disposable income could lower to the point where a planned increase in savings could actually reduce savings. With savings increased at the expense of consumption, a decrease in consumption will decrease aggregate demand. With aggregate demand decreasing, businesses will not be able to sell as much output. This will further lower investment, output, and jobs. Incomes will decrease as a result. As incomes decrease, consumers will have less disposable income, less money available for both consumption and savings. The actual amount of savings can thus be decreased due to a planned increase in savings. This is the paradox of thrift.

The paradox of thrift is actually a fallacy of composition.

The decision to increase savings is an individual decision, made on a microeconomic level. The individual can increase savings by personal choice. The resulting decrease in savings from the paradox of thrift is a macroeconomic result, the cumulative outcome of individual actions. Savings may decrease in the overall economy, for savers in general, not necessarily for any specific individual who chose to increase savings.

The paradox of thrift can be shown graphically on a diagram of leakages and injections into the circular flow model of GDP. For this purpose, leakages can be considered to be savings, while injections can be considered to be investment. Such a diagram would have the level of savings / investment on the vertical axis, and the level of income (or real GDP) on the horizontal axis.

The savings (leakages) curve would slope upward. Normally, the investment (injections) curve would slope downward. Equilibrium is where these two curves intersect. An increase in the MPS would be shown as an upward (leftward, not rightward) shift in the savings curve. A resulting increase in investment would be shown as an upward (and rightward) shift in the investment curve. The two shifts together would result in an increase in real GDP.

But with the paradox of thrift, the resulting increase in investment would not occur. This would be shown as a horizontal, not a downward sloping, investment curve. An upward shift in the savings curve, combined with no shift in the horizontal investment curve, would result in a decrease in real GDP.

Fiscal and Monetary Policies

Governments have three sources of funds to pay for expenditures: printing money, borrowing money, and collecting taxes. In the United States, only the federal government is allowed to print money. Also, state and local governments in the United States are limited by law in the types of borrowing and taxation that they are allowed to use.

Fiscal and monetary policies are involved in every aspect of the operation of governments. These policies are often thought of in terms of discretionary policies. Discretionary fiscal and monetary policies involve government's active role in the economy in an attempt to create a specific outcome.

Economic growth, employment, and stable prices are goals that fiscal and monetary policies attempt to achieve. In the United States, these goals have been codified into law with the Employment Act of 1946. Discretionary fiscal and monetary policies can be used to achieve other outcomes as well. Wealth distribution, market failures, and infrastructure are among the possible targets of government policy. Infrastructure refers to a nation's basic public institutions and facilities, including an education system and a system of roads and bridges.

Fiscal policy is the policy of the government relating to government spending and taxing decisions. The entire budget of the government is the result of fiscal policy. Fiscal policy affects the economy's total output (real GDP) and price level because it affects aggregate demand both directly and indirectly. Because fiscal policy can change aggregate demand, it has been called demand side economics, or Keynesian Economics.

Fiscal policy includes components that are discretionary in nature. Discretionary fiscal policies are policies that are designed to achieve specific economic outcomes, such as decreasing unemployment. Discretionary fiscal policies are deliberate government interventions in the economy.

Fiscal policy also includes automatic stabilizers. These are policies that kick in whenever aggregate income changes. Automatic stabilizers work to offset the effects of changes in income. For example, unemployment compensation will partially offset the loss of income, and the associated loss of consumer demand, when people lose jobs. When the unemployment rate increases, so does the aggregate amount of unemployment compensation paid by the government. Similar types of automatic stabilizers are welfare payments and food stamps.

These automatic stabilizers are transfer payments. Transfer payments represent money that government collects in taxes from one group of people and pays out in benefits to another group of people. Since transfer payments do not represent government purchases of goods and services, and do not reflect current production, they are not included in GDP.

Transfer payments do not affect aggregate demand directly, but they do change aggregate demand indirectly through changes in disposable income. For example, if the transfer is from a group with a low MPC (people who tend to save a relatively large portion of their disposable income) to a group with a high MPC (people who tend to spend a relatively large portion of their disposable income), then aggregate consumption spending will increase.

Another type of automatic stabilizer is a progressive income tax. When incomes fall, taxpayers are moved to a lower tax bracket. The amount of taxes collected from income falls. This partially offsets the loss of disposable income by taking less in taxes out of personal income. This helps to offset the decrease in consumption spending caused by a recession.

The remainder of this section on fiscal policy focuses primarily on discretionary fiscal policy.

Government Spending:

Government purchases (but not transfer payments) are part of real GDP. They are the "G" in the formula $GDP=C+I+G+(X-M)$. Government purchases form an autonomous portion of aggregate demand. Government spending is not affected by the price level, but it can change the equilibrium price level. A change in government spending will shift the aggregate demand curve.

If a recessionary gap exists, equilibrium real GDP is below potential real GDP. The amount by which real GDP is below potential GDP is called a GDP gap. An increase in government spending can shift the aggregate demand curve to the right, increasing equilibrium real GDP towards the level of potential real GDP, closing the GDP gap.

How much does government spending have to increase in order to eliminate a recessionary gap? With an upward sloping aggregate supply curve, won't part of the increase in government spending simply go towards higher prices instead of higher real output?

The answers to these questions depend on factors that determine the effectiveness of discretionary fiscal policy.

Discretionary fiscal policy can influence the level of aggregate demand, and real output, both directly and indirectly. The effectiveness of fiscal policy in achieving policy goals depends on a number of factors, including the slope of the aggregate supply curve, the magnitude of the multiplier effect, and the government's chosen method for financing the associated expenditures.

The slope of the aggregate supply curve:

John Maynard Keynes developed the aggregate demand and aggregate supply model by holding the price level constant. In effect, he assumed an aggregate supply curve that is a horizontal line set at a given price level. The level of real GDP, then, would depend entirely on aggregate demand.

This assumption is not entirely unrealistic for what Keynes was trying to show. Keynes was dealing with the Great Depression. He was trying to show why the self-correcting mechanism of classical economic theory did not kick in to fix the economy. Classical economic theory could not explain the magnitude or the length of the Great Depression. Keynes developed a theory to both explain why the classical theory did not work, and to show how fiscal policy could work to end the Great Depression.

By holding the price level constant, the relationship between aggregate demand and real output is emphasized. Keynes' theory emphasized that wages and prices are not free to adjust downward. In his model, wages and prices will not adjust upward either during recessionary times.

Evidence seems to suggest that when real GDP is well below potential GDP, an increase in aggregate demand will have little effect on the price level. This means that the aggregate supply curve is mostly flat (horizontal) in recessionary times. But as output increases, the aggregate supply curve steepens. An increase in government spending to stimulate aggregate demand will be more effective in increasing real GDP during a recession but more inflationary as real GDP nears potential GDP. This can be explained, at least in part, by the fact that more excess capacity exists during a recession. When many unemployed workers are available, and equipment and land sit idle, then output can be increased without putting upward pressure on prices in the factor markets. But when excess capacity is not available, then output can only be increased by bidding up prices in the factor markets.

The multiplier effect:

Government spending is an autonomous portion of aggregate demand. Its effect on the economy, however, may be more than the original amount of government spending. This is because government purchases become income for somebody in the economy (refer to the circular flow model). A portion of this income will be spent, creating income for somebody else; and this process continues to multiply throughout the economy.

How much is the multiplier effect? This can be shown with a simple mathematical formula.

Recall that in the circular flow model, leakages and injections exist. Leakages are savings, taxes, and imports. Injections are investments, government purchases, and exports. In equilibrium, total leakages equal total injections. Taxes which are used to finance government spending will have their own offsetting multiplier effect. The rest of the leakages and injections are incorporated into the formula:

Spending multiplier = 1 / leakages = 1 / (MPS + MPI)

In this formula, MPS is the fraction of new income that will be saved instead of being spent, and MPI is the fraction of new income that will be spent on imports, or goods that are not produced domestically. The amount that government spending would have to increase in order to close a GDP gap is called a recessionary gap. A recessionary gap is equal to the GDP gap divided by the spending multiplier.

Consumers have two choices when it comes to disposable income: they can either spend it or they can save it. The portion of disposable income that consumers spend goes directly into consumption spending (the "C" portion of the calculation of GDP), increasing aggregate demand and GDP, as well as keeping the money in the circular flow. The portion of disposable income that consumers save becomes a leakage in the circular flow. It is not subject to the multiplier effect. When disposable income increases, the portion of the increase that is spent is called the marginal propensity to consume (MPC). The portion of the increase that is saved is called the marginal propensity to save (MPS). Both are measured as a fraction of disposable income. Together, the portion of an increase in disposable income that is spent and the portion that is saved will equal the total increase, so that MPC plus MPS equals one. Since these are marginal measurements, they can change as the level of income changes. For example, a consumer with a very low income will likely spend a relatively high proportion of a given increase in income. A consumer with a very high income will likely spend a relatively low proportion of the same increase in income.

Methods of financing government purchases:

Governments have three methods of raising funds to pay for purchases: taxing, borrowing, and printing money.

Government purchases financed by taxing:

An increase in taxes decreases disposable income, which decreases consumption spending. This is a decrease in aggregate demand that will offset the increase in aggregate demand created by an increase in government spending, but only partially.

The reason that the increase in aggregate demand caused by government spending is greater than the decrease in aggregate demand caused by taxes: not all taxes will be paid for with a decrease in consumption. A portion of an increase in taxes will be paid for with a decrease in savings. The net effect is that aggregate demand will increase by the marginal propensity to save (MPS).

An increase in taxes may also decrease aggregate supply. With a smaller disposable income, the incentive to work will be lower. The opportunity cost of time away from work will decrease. If an increase in taxes causes the amount of labor input to decrease, then a decrease in aggregate supply will result. This will offset, at least partially, any gains in real GDP caused by an increase in government spending.

This will also create inflation, based on the slopes of the aggregate supply and aggregate demand curves. The magnitude of the effect that an increase in taxes has on aggregate supply is open to debate. Supply-side economists believe that this effect is very significant. Keynesian economists believe that it is insignificant.

Government purchases financed by borrowing:

Governments borrow money by selling government bonds in the open market. To the purchasers of the bonds, this represents a financial investment. To the government that issues the bonds, this represents a loan that has to be repaid. Each bond has specified dates in which the government must make interest and principle payments to the investor. When these payments come due, the government can choose to finance the payments by issuing new bonds. Of course, this would be additional deficit spending that increases the national debt.

Eventually, the money that the government borrows must be paid for with tax collections. A few economists believe that consumers will take these future tax payments into consideration when making spending decisions. They will reduce consumption, and put money into savings in order to pay for a future tax increase that has yet to be announced. This concept is called the Ricardian Equivalence. The effect of borrowing on aggregate demand would be the same as the effect of a tax increase. Most economists do not believe that the Ricardian Equivalence holds true.

Government borrowing can also reduce aggregate demand due to crowding out of private investment. Crowding out is a term that refers to a reduction in consumption or private investment caused by an increase in the government's debt. A sale of government bonds is often large enough to influence the market price in the overall bond market. A large increase in the supply of bonds will decrease the prices of all bonds in the market. Lower bond prices mean higher interest rates. An increase in interest rates will increase the cost of borrowing for private firms. Since most private investment is financed with borrowed funds, an increase in interest rates will increase the cost of investment spending and reduce the profitability of investment projects. This will reduce the amount of private investment spending, and aggregate demand.

The evidence for the crowding out effect is inconclusive. Considerable disagreements exist among economists regarding its importance.

Government purchases financed by printing money:

Financing government expenditures with new money involves monetary policy. Monetary policy is an alternative to discretionary fiscal policy for governments to influence real output and price levels. In the United States, monetary policy is conducted independently from fiscal policy.

Much disagreement exists among economists as to the relative effectiveness of monetary policy vs. fiscal policy, the relative effectiveness of specific policy tools, and the wisdom of using these tools in the first place. These different opinions are the reason why different economics schools of thought exist. These different opinions also constitute a sizable portion of different political positions.

Different countries have different monetary and banking systems. The discussion in this section will be based on the tools of monetary policy within the United States' Federal Reserve System (the Fed).

The Fed has a degree of power to control the money supply in the economy. The level of the money supply influences the level of real GDP as well as the price level. The tools that the Fed uses to control the money supply are: open market operations, changes in the reserve requirement, and changes in the discount rate.

Open market operations:

The main tool used by the Fed to control the money supply is the use of open market operations. This tool involves the Fed buying or selling government bonds on the open market.

If the Fed wants to increase the money supply, it will buy government bonds on the open market. When the Fed buys bonds, the money paid for the bonds is deposited into the accounts of brokers at various commercial banks. These deposits become new additions to the money supply and new excess reserves for the banks to lend out. This makes the amount spent on the purchase of bonds subject to the money multiplier.

Banks sometimes borrow overnight funds from each other in order to cover deficiencies in reserves caused by unexpected withdrawals. The rate that they charge each other is called the federal funds rate. With an increase in excess reserves in the banking system caused by the Fed buying bonds, the cost of borrowing for banks becomes lower. This lowers the federal funds rate. A lower federal funds rate decreases bank costs, and banks can charge lower interest rates to their borrowing customers. This in turn lowers the cost of private business investment, resulting in more investment spending in the economy.

If the Fed wants to decrease the money supply, the opposite occurs. The Fed sells bonds, and the money it receives from the proceeds is deducted from the broker accounts. This decreases the money supply, excess reserves, and the amount of reserves subject to the money multiplier. This also increases the federal funds rate and commercial interest rates, decreasing investment spending.

The Fed compares the federal funds rate to a target rate in order to determine when to engage in open market operations.

Open market operations can also influence long term bond rates to move in the same direction as the overnight (short term) federal funds rate. When the Fed buys bonds, its actions increase the demand for bonds. With the laws of supply and demand in effect, an increase in the demand for bonds will increase the prices of bonds on the open market. An increase in the prices of bonds will decrease their yields, or interest rates. When the Fed sells bonds, it increases the supply of bonds. This decreases the prices of bonds, increasing their interest rates.

The Fed is able to influence bond rates because of market power. Transactions by the Fed can be a relatively large portion of the overall bond market. In addition, the Fed theoretically makes open market decisions without regard for any profit motive, but competes in the bond market with investors who are guided by profits.

The "government bonds" in this discussion of open market operations refers to Treasury securities. These include Treasury Bills (T-Bills), which are short term instruments that mature in less than one year; Treasury Notes (T-Notes), which are bonds that mature within one to ten years; and Treasury Bonds (T-Bonds), which are long term bonds that mature in twenty to thirty years.

Treasury Bills have no specified interest amount or rate attached to them. Instead, T-Bills are issued at a discount from par value, and pay the full par value upon maturity. The amount of interest income received by an investor in T-Bills would be the difference between the proceeds upon sale or maturity and the initial cost to the investor. The government's interest expense for T-Bills would be the difference between the amount paid to investors at maturity and the proceeds received by the government upon issue. The interest rate would be the interest amount as a percentage of the cost.

Treasury Notes and Treasury Bonds pay interest based on a stated percentage of face or par value. This percentage or interest rate is annualized, with payments made every six months. The full par value is paid upon maturity.

Changes in the reserve requirement:

When the reserve requirement increases, excess reserves decrease. This decreases the amount of reserves available for banks to loan out. This in turn decreases the ability of individual commercial banks to create new money. This decreases the amount of money subject to the deposit expansion multiplier. When the reserve requirement decreases, excess reserves increase, new money created from bank loans increases, and the amount of money subject to the deposit expansion multiplier increases.

Changes in the discount rate:

The discount rate affects the money supply in the same way that the federal funds rate does. The difference is that the federal funds rate is a market interest rate that banks use to borrow funds from each other, while the discount rate is an interest rate that the Fed sets for funds that banks borrow directly from the Fed.

The discount rate is slightly higher than the federal funds rate. The Fed actually uses two different discount rates. It charges a lower rate to banks in good financial condition (banks with high credit ratings). This lower discount rate is the lowest interest rate that the Fed has direct control over.

In certain situations, the use of monetary policy to influence the economy might be ineffective. Liquidity Trap is the theory that expansionary monetary policy may be ineffective after a certain point. The liquidity trap theory states that when nominal interest rates are close to zero, monetary policy tools are ineffective in lowering them further. This theory is often associated with expected deflation.

When the economy is in a recession, without the presence of a liquidity trap, monetary policy can be used in order to try to increase private business investment. The cost of investment is interest, and an increase in investment spending can increase output, jobs, and income. Monetary policy during recessionary times would involve lowering interest rates.

However, if prices are expected to fall, then the nominal interest rate is lower than the real interest rate. The nominal interest rate is equal to the real rate plus expected inflation. Expected deflation will cause the nominal rate to be lower than the real rate. The lower limit for nominal interest rates is zero (because if the nominal interest rate were less than zero, it would mean that creditors would be paying debtors for the use of the creditors' money, which wouldn't make sense).

Therefore, nominal rates cannot fall below zero. With expected deflation, and nominal interest rates lower than real interest rates, a real interest rate would exist that cannot be reduced with the use of monetary policy; the lower limit would prevent a further reduction. When interest rates cannot be lowered using monetary policy, then monetary policy cannot be effective in increasing investment, output, jobs, and income. This is the liquidity trap.

The tools of monetary policy used by the Fed are designed to control the money supply. But the goal of monetary policy is to influence the level of real output (real GDP) and the price level, not the money supply. How does the money supply affect these primary goals? The answer is that the size and growth of the money supply is an intermediate target.

The relationship between the intermediate target of the money supply and the goals of output and stable prices can be explained by showing how changes in the money supply affect the aggregate demand and aggregate supply model.

Start with the demand for money. People hold money balances in order to pay for transactions (the transaction demand for money); to be prepared for emergencies (the precautionary demand for money); and as a hedge against price changes in other financial assets (the speculative demand for money).

The amount of money that people want to hold for these purposes depends on the interest rate and nominal income. When interest rates increase, so does the value of holding assets that pay more in income than money deposits. The opportunity cost of holding money increases. Therefore, an inverse relationship exists between interest rates and the demand for money.

A direct relationship exists between nominal income and the demand for money. Money is needed to finance transactions, and at higher nominal levels the value of transactions increases. Either the higher nominal income will mean higher real income, in which case consumers will purchase more goods and services in order to increase their standard of living; or higher nominal income will mean higher prices, in which case consumers will spend more income for the same amount of goods and services.

A graph showing the demand for money will be a downward sloping curve with the interest rate on the price (vertical) axis and the quantity of money demanded on the horizontal axis. As interest rates change, the quantity of money demanded will move up and down the money demand curve. As nominal income changes, the quantity of money demanded will change at every interest rate level, and the money demand curve will shift.

The supply of money is controlled by the Fed. The money supply curve is a vertical line at the level of the money supply set by the Fed. When the money demand curve and the money supply curve are combined on one graph, equilibrium will be at the point where these two curves intersect. The equilibrium quantity of money will be the quantity set by the Fed. The equilibrium interest rate will be the interest rate where the money demand curve crosses the equilibrium quantity of money.

Finally, all of this information can be incorporated into the aggregate demand and aggregate supply model to show the relationship between the money supply, output, and the price level.

Notice from the explanation that with different monetary policy tools, an inverse relationship exists between the money supply and the interest rate. Also, an inverse relationship exists between the interest rate and the level of private investment. Since private investment is a portion of aggregate demand, a positive relationship exists between the money supply and aggregate demand.

The larger the money supply, the higher the aggregate demand. This relationship is what the Fed relies on when it decides to use its monetary policy tools. As aggregate demand increases, equilibrium real output (real GDP) increases and the equilibrium price level increases. The magnitude of each increase is subject to debate, and depends on the slopes of the aggregate demand and aggregate supply curves.

Some economic schools of thought argue that an increase in the money supply is mostly inflationary. Other schools of thought argue that an increase in the money supply will mostly increase real output. Evidence is unclear, but seems to suggest that an increase in the money supply becomes more inflationary as equilibrium real GDP increases and nears potential real GDP. This affects the relationship between inflation and unemployment.

Also, large increases in the money supply in a short period of time can possibly cause a jolt to the economy and become inflationary as well.

Deficits and the National Debt

Many people are confused about the difference between a deficit and a debt. A deficit refers to an excess of expenditures over revenue during a specific time period. The national deficit usually refers to the amount by which government spending is in excess of tax revenue in a given year. This is a flow concept. It involves activity over a period of time. A debt refers to the balance of all funds owed from prior commitments. The national debt refers to the balance of all payments owed at a given point in time due to previous deficit spending. The national debt is the total amount of government bonds outstanding. Essentially, it is a running total of previous deficits, less payments made on prior debts. This is a stock concept. It involves a balance at a specific point in time.

Both national deficits and national debts are created by borrowing instead of using tax revenue to pay for government expenditures. Governments borrow money by issuing government bonds to the public. These government bonds represent financial investments to the purchasers, but for the government that issued the bond they represent an obligation that must be repaid.

One measure of the national debt is the percentage of debt to GDP. This measure serves as a reference point. It will put the debt into perspective as to the size of the economy.

Consequences of deficits and the national debt:

Potential consequences of government debt include crowding out, trade deficits, and interest payments as an obligation in future government budgets.

Crowding out:

It is not entirely clear that crowding out occurs, so differences of opinions exist among economists from different schools of thought. If crowding out indeed occurs, it does so through this process:

When a government runs a deficit, it finances expenditures through borrowing. This involves selling bonds on the open market. When the government sells bonds, it increases the supply of bonds, decreasing the market price of all bonds on the market. It can influence the market prices because the government's transactions are often a large percentage of the activity in the bond market, giving the government market power. When bond prices decrease, their yields increase, raising the interest rates for bonds. If this in turn causes other interest rates in the economy to increase, then the cost of borrowing will increase for firms planning private investment. If firms decrease investments due to higher interest rates, and these higher interest rates are in turn caused by government deficits (the federal deficit), then private investments are "crowded out". This will decrease real GDP both in the present time period and in the future. This scenario cannot take place during a liquidity trap. The process of crowding out requires increasing interest rates, something that doesn't occur during a liquidity trap.

Trade deficits:

Some economists believe that budget deficits lead to trade deficits. If budget deficits do indeed raise real interest rates and cause crowding out, then domestic securities will be more attractive to foreign investors. If foreign investors buy more domestic securities as a result, this will increase demand for the domestic currency. The domestic currency will appreciate in value due to an increase in demand. This changes the exchange rates for currencies, making foreign-made goods cheaper for domestic consumers and domestic-made goods more expensive for foreign consumers. As a result, net exports will decrease, which will also decrease real GDP.

Interest payments as an obligation in future government budgets:

The national debt requires the government to make interest payments in the future. These interest payments represent money that the government cannot use for something else, including tax relief. To the extent that these payments are made to domestic investors, and are paid for with taxes collected from domestic taxpayers, the immediate net change in national wealth would be zero. This has been called "owing money to ourselves". This would, however, have a redistribution effect, which could affect future real GDP in a number of ways. Wealth would be redistributed from the taxpayer class to the investor class.

To the extent that these interest payments are made to foreign investors, they represent wealth leaving the domestic economy. This would be a reduction in the domestic standard of living. In this sense, having foreigners own government bonds, and therefore a sizeable portion of the national debt, becomes a real issue, not just political rhetoric.

However, the real effect of foreign ownership of domestic government bonds needs to be evaluated in terms of opportunity costs. If the money received from selling bonds to foreigners allowed for an increase in domestic output that would not have occurred otherwise, this creates a benefit of having foreign ownership of government debt. This benefit may very well outweigh the loss of wealth created later when the interest payments leave the country.

Short run vs. long run deficits:

Some government deficits are caused by fiscal policies that are designed to offset the negative consequences of the business cycle. Many of these policies fall into the category of automatic stabilizers, which mean that they are not related to current policy decisions, but rather are the result of ongoing stabilizing policies created in the past. When unemployment is high, and output (real GDP) is low, then tax revenue will decrease, which will partially offset the decrease in disposable income caused by a recession. To the extent that this affects the classes with a high MPC, the economic recovery can be aided with the use of a progressive income tax structure. Increased transfer payments caused by an increase in the number of people who qualify for public assistance such as unemployment insurance benefits and welfare are also automatic stabilizers. These automatic deficits are considered to be short term deficits, because they will automatically decrease when the economy gains strength. Besides automatic stabilizers, other forms of stabilizers that result in short run deficits include things like one time only economic stimulus plans.

Deficits caused by policies that are unrelated to the business cycle are considered to be long term deficits. If the short run stabilizer-type deficits succeed in aiding economic recovery, they can reduce long term deficit spending.

Globalization

The many nations of the world, and their economies, have become increasingly inter-related in recent years. This trend is only expected to grow. This trend has led to the term "global economy". Technology is a driving force for increased globalization. Global markets have developed as a result of rapid advances in communications and transportation.

Global trade is a hot political issue. Understanding the economic concepts included here will help you to understand the political arguments relating to trade. Hopefully, you will be able to understand what the politicians are saying about global trade and whether their arguments are valid or not. The issues are complicated. Any given policy is likely to benefit one segment of the economy while hurting another segment. In that case, weighing the costs and benefits of one policy choice against another requires value judgments. The value judgments are not included here. Value judgments violate "economic thinking" through the use of normative rather than positive statements, taking the issue past the realm of economics into the realm of politics.

The information included here is based entirely on economics concepts: it is not biased towards one policy or another. But a well-informed voter intent on making unbiased value judgments can use this information to understand what really is involved with these issues. Then, any value judgments at least will be based on sound economic principles. An unbiased voter will want to support policies that will have the desired outcomes.

This chapter is limited to basic concepts behind the complexities of globalization rather than dealing with all of the complexities themselves. Three broad categories of topics related to globalization are included: foreign exchange, balance of payments, and trade restrictions.

Foreign exchange:

When a buyer in one country purchases a good or service from a supplier in another country, the exchange that takes place is paid for in the currency of the seller's country. The buyer needs to have the currency of the seller in order to make the purchase. This can be in the form of the physical currency of the seller, but most often such an exchange would take place using an electronic transfer of funds to an account valued in that currency. The physical transfer of one currency to another, in other words buying foreign paper money or coins occurs mostly for the purpose of tourism. Either way, transferring funds from one currency to another involves the foreign exchange market.

The definition of a foreign exchange market: a global market in which people trade one currency for another.

The foreign exchange market is not a physical market located in a specific location. It is a global market located throughout the world, often involving electronic transfers through large banks. When funds valued in one currency are exchanged for funds valued in another currency, the relative value of one currency in terms of the other currency determines the amounts of currencies that are exchanged. This creates a price for the two currencies in terms of each other: the price is called the exchange rate.

Exchange rates are determined by relative values, so they can be found by dividing a specific quantity of one currency by a quantity of equal value of the other currency. Once you know the exchange rate, you can translate a specific amount of one currency to the equivalent amount of another currency either by multiplying or dividing one currency's quantity by the exchange rate. Whether you have to multiply or divide depends on which way the exchange rate is quoted: if it is quoted as currency A in terms of currency B, or currency B in terms of currency A.

Many exchange rates have a standard method used for reporting purposes: for example, always currency A in terms of currency B, not currency B in terms of currency A. There are many different currencies in the world that can be exchanged for one another. This means that for a given country's currency, a list of exchange rates that includes standard reporting methods would include some that require multiplication, and some that require division.

The foreign exchange market works just like any other market in the sense that prices are determined by supply and demand. In the case of the foreign exchange market, it means that exchange rates are determined by the supply and demand for currencies. One currency appreciates in value when its value rises in relation to another currency, and depreciates in value when its value falls in relation to another currency.

Since goods and services sold for export involve an exchange of currencies, the exchange rate will affect the price that consumers have to pay for imports. This means that goods and services in one country can become relatively more or less expensive than goods and services in another country, due only to a change in the exchange rate between the two currencies. When a country's currency appreciates in value against another currency, that country's goods and services become more expensive for the other country's citizens. When a country's currency depreciates in value against another currency, that country's goods and services become less expensive for the other country's citizens.

With increasing globalization, supply and demand forces mean that currency exchange rate changes will alter a country's balance of trade. An appreciated currency will create fewer exports and more imports, decreasing the balance of trade and real GDP. The reciprocal: a depreciated currency will create more exports and fewer imports, increasing the balance of trade and real GDP.

Balance of payments:

Balance of payments is not the same thing as balance of trade. Balance of payments refers to a record of a country's trade with the rest of the world. This record includes transactions involving accounts in goods, services, and financial assets. Balance of trade involves only one such account, as explained below. Balance of payments, by definition, must always be zero: debits equal credits. Each transaction involves an equal amount of something received and something given up. If someone mentions a surplus or deficit in the balance of payments, they are really talking about something else. The use of such terminology can be misleading.

The balance of payments is divided into two broad categories: the current account and the financial account.

The current account in turn is divided into four categories: the merchandise account, the services account, the income account, and the unilateral transfers account. Each of these accounts can carry a surplus or a deficit balance, and so can their sum (the balance of the current account).

A brief description of each of these four accounts:

The merchandise account includes transactions involving goods traded between countries. The export of a good would be a positive (credit) entry in the merchandise account. The import of a good would be a negative (debit) entry in the merchandise account. The merchandise account is important because exports represent production for the domestic economy, while imports represent spending on goods that are not part of domestic production. Exports represent activity within the economy, including jobs, business creation, and economic growth. Imports represent goods that have been purchased from potential competitors of domestic producers, which would mean a loss of jobs, business, economic growth.

This is important politically, especially when the political concern is loss of jobs and business within specific sectors of the economy (such as manufacturing), or entire industries. This political concern is one of the main considerations whenever trade barriers are being considered. On the other hand, at least theoretically, imports represent goods that can be produced more efficiently elsewhere, so that domestic resources can be re-allocated to more efficient uses. This re-allocation of resources means that the overall economy can produce more with the same amount of resources. The result is more, not less, business, economic growth, and jobs.

So, the merchandise account is an example of economic forces that decrease economic activity in one sense while increasing economic activity in another sense. How a person interprets this discrepancy will likely influence which policies that person will support.

Balance of trade usually refers to the balance in the merchandise account.

The services account includes transactions between countries involving services. This account includes tourism and transaction costs, such as transportation costs for merchandise transactions.

The income account includes transactions involving income between countries. Investment income and wages earned in another country is a positive (credit). Investment income and wages earned from domestic activity by foreigners would be a negative (debit).

The unilateral transfers account includes transactions between countries in which only one country actually receives something. This would include gifts and pensions. This account has political implications, especially regarding immigration policy. A foreign national who earns money in the domestic economy but sends some of the money earned to family members in another country would be creating a negative (debit) in the unilateral transfers account.

The merchandise account comprises by far the largest portion of the current account. For this reason, both the current account balance and the merchandise account balance are sometimes referred to as the balance of trade.

Recall that the balance of payments includes both the current account and the financial account. The financial account represents the flow of money between countries. It basically includes the other side of the entries in the current account. For example, exports would mean that goods are transferred out of the country, but an equal value of money is transferred into the country. The flow of goods would be reflected in the current account while the flow of money would be reflected in the financial account.

Every transaction involves an equal value of credits and debits. This means that if either the current account or the financial account reflects a surplus, the other one must reflect a deficit of the same amount.

What all of this means in terms of GDP, debt, and political implications:

Recall that when calculating GDP, exports are added and imports are subtracted. Exports represent production that is produced domestically but not consumed domestically. Imports represent domestic consumption that does not add to production, so imports have to be subtracted when computing GDP in order to reflect production.

When the value of exports and imports are not equal, then consumption does not equal production. The difference between the two represents borrowing. If imports are greater than exports, indicated by a debit balance in the current account and a credit balance in the financial account, then the country is a net debtor nation. It borrows more money from the rest of the world than it loans to the rest of the world. If exports are greater than imports, the country is a net creditor nation. This has political implications, as debt implies money owed.

A trade deficit is not the same thing as the national debt, although politicians often imply that it is. A trade deficit is a net debit in the current account of the balance of payments. The national debt is a completely different concept: it represents the total outstanding balance of all government obligations to pay back creditors, which in reality are investors in government securities.

The United States was a net creditor nation prior to 1985, even though it had a large national debt. Since 1985, both the national debt and the balance of trade deficit have increased, and the United States has become the largest net debtor nation in the world.

Trade restrictions:

Trade restrictions generally refer to the various barriers to free trade (imports and exports) imposed by governments. Different reasons have been given for restricting trade. Among them are:

National security: Governments often determine that restricting the export or import of specific products is in the national best interest. A nation that produces weapons systems may want to prohibit those systems from being sold to potential enemies of the state. Some products may be deemed to be vital to the well-being of the country. The government doesn't want to rely on imports for a significant portion of the nation's supply, even if imports are less expensive than domestic production.

Infant industry: Sometimes governments believe that specific industries which are less efficient than foreign competition would become more efficient if given time to develop without being undermined by cheaper foreign prices. This is based on the idea that new industries tend to have high startup costs, but the costs will decrease if the industry has time to develop. Without protection, these companies cannot survive long enough to realize such cost savings.

Retaliation: The argument for this is that "if they impose restrictions on us, we should impose restrictions on them in order to level the playing field, in order to make trade fair".

Jobs protection: If jobs are "shipped overseas", then domestic unemployment increases. Evidence shows that trade restrictions to protect jobs can increase employment in protected industries, but will not increase employment in the overall economy. The job gains in the protected industries would be offset by job losses in perhaps more efficient industries. This would indicate that this argument may be more valid in terms of national interest than in terms of jobs.

Low foreign wages: Countries with a lower standard of living tend to pay lower wages. This is often true when comparing developing nations with established industrialized nations. Some countries have few laws to protect workers, such as minimum wage, working conditions, and child labor laws. With lower labor costs, businesses and especially manufacturing businesses will be able to produce more efficiently if they produce in a foreign country. One offsetting argument to this is that efficiency may not be real if the foreign workers are less productive than the domestic workers, who may be more educated, better trained, etc.

Politics: Politicians may find it desirable to bow to pressure from special interests, and protect specific industries located in their districts. This protection wouldn't necessarily be based on national security, infant industry, or other arguments. It would, however, give special treatment to specific industries over other industries.

Types of trade barriers include tariffs, import quotas, embargoes, subsidies, purchase restrictions, product standards, voluntary export restrictions, and anti-dumping laws.

A tariff is a tax on imported goods. It increases the cost of imports in the domestic market, making domestic production relatively less costly than it would be without the tariff. This will decrease imports and increase domestic production in a protected industry. The existence of imports in an industry is an indication that at the current level of domestic demand, foreign production is more efficient than domestic production. With a tariff restricting imports, the domestic consumer will have to pay a higher price, and receive a smaller level of output. The domestic producers in the protected industry will gain from a tariff because it will allow them to increase prices and output.

Those who gain from a tariff: domestic producers and the government (tax revenue). Those who lose: domestic consumers and foreign producers.

Import quotas restrict the amount of imports to a specific level. Once that level is reached, additional domestic demand will have to be met by domestic producers. This will mean that if demand increases, domestic consumers will not have the benefit of the cheaper world price (the world price necessarily would be lower than its domestic counterpart if an import quota is to be effective). All of the additional production to meet an increase in demand will be met by domestic producers.

Winners and losers with import quotas are similar to the situation with tariffs, except that import quotas do not provide revenue for the government.

An embargo is similar to an import quota, except that it restricts all imports for a specific product, or for a specific industry, or from a specific country. In effect, it is an import quota of zero.

A subsidy is a payment that the government makes to domestic producers of products that are produced for export. A subsidy basically lowers the cost of production for domestic producers, making it more profitable for them to sell their products relative to foreign competition. Subsidies are sometimes referred to as negative taxes.

Purchase restrictions occur when governments pass laws limiting themselves to purchase from domestic producers.

The government can require goods sold domestically to meet specific safety standards that are above the standards of the country that exports to the domestic market. This will mean that the exporter will either have to quit selling to the country that enacts such standards, leaving the domestic producer with less competition, or raise their standards for the products that they wish to export. This would increase their costs, and make them relatively less efficient than before such standards.

A voluntary export restriction is the same thing as a quota, but without a specific law to mandate enforcement. It amounts to an agreement by a nation to limit the amount that it exports to a specific country. The reason countries would do such a thing voluntarily is because of an implied threat of retaliation. This means that such restrictions are not completely voluntary.

An anti-dumping law is the other side of a subsidy. A country pays a subsidy so its producers can export to the world at a lower cost. An anti-dumping law would be the retaliation from the importer, to restrict the imports of goods that it deems are sold on the world market at unfairly low prices because of subsidies that another country pays its producers.

Economic Schools of Thought

What follows is a brief historical overview of some of the teachings of the Classical, Keynesian, and Monetarist schools. This is not a comprehensive list of all differences. This overview does not include all arguments made by different schools of thought. It includes the major schools of thought that historically have dominated economic thinking, but does not include every modern economic school of thought.

What is included in this chapter should give readers a general idea of the thought processes used by advocates of different points of view. This overview does include some of the terminology of economics that can be found in various places throughout this book.

Philosophy of macroeconomic policy for the past several decades is generally thought of as being a clash between two distinct points of view, Keynesian and Monetarist. The viewpoints of Keynesians and Monetarists both have evolved over the years, and the result of this evolution has led to some confusion and misinformation about what the viewpoints actually are. I believe that a brief description of the historical evolution of these points of view will help clear up this confusion. More importantly, a study of how the different viewpoints developed over the years will go a long way towards learning what the current debate is all about. Learning the history behind the debate is probably the best way to learn what the debate is about. So this analysis begins with the historical background:

The Keynesian school of thought began with John Maynard Keynes, who developed an alternative to the Classical economic school as a result of the realities of the Great Depression in the 1930s.

Classical economists had believed that an output level below the full-employment level, which is the case during a recession, is not a position of equilibrium, and that market forces would bring the economy back to the full-employment level. This is the self-correcting nature of laissez-faire economics. No government intervention in the economy is needed because the economy will shortly correct itself. This self-correction involves the following process, according to classical economists:

The unemployment created by a recession means that an excess labor supply exists in the economy. This excess labor supply will drive down the wage rates, and lower aggregate demand will drive down the overall price level. With lower prices, consumers will have more real wealth in terms of purchasing power, and will increase consumption spending. This change in real wealth is called the wealth effect. As consumption spending increases, aggregate demand in the economy will increase until the full-employment level of output is reached. There is no need for government interference in the economy because the economy will correct itself.

During the Great Depression of the 1930s, however, it became obvious that this self-correcting mechanism did not kick in. The economies of nations around the world remained, for a long period of time, at a level far below the full-employment level. This meant that either equilibrium was reached at below full employment, in which case the economy would never correct itself; or the self-correcting mechanism would take much too long and cause too much damage to be acceptable to society. Keynes came along with his own economic theories to explain this. He published them in a book entitled **THE GENERAL THEORY OF EMPLOYMENT, INTEREST, AND MONEY**, in 1936.

Keynes believed that the classical theory was incorrect. He believed that wages and prices were resistant to downward pressure, so that the self-correcting mechanism could not kick in. In the classical view, lower wages and prices are the necessary incentive for self-correction. Indeed, ever since Keynes' time, historical events have shown that wages and prices are indeed resistant to downward pressures. Since this self-correction would not occur, Keynes advocated government intervention, but only during times when the economy was in a recession or a depression. His advice was strong fiscal and monetary policies in order to correct the economy. He believed that fiscal policies (lower taxes, increased government spending) and monetary policies (controlling the money supply and interest rates through the use of various central banking actions) were both effective. But he believed that fiscal policies were more effective than monetary policies.

Other notable beliefs of Keynes: Mild inflation would redistribute wealth from the "idle" classes to the "active" classes, including businesses. This would ensure a healthy level of business profits. These profits would in turn be available for investment, which would create economic growth. But Keynes also believed that business confidence was extremely volatile and unpredictable, causing investment spending to fluctuate. Keynes also believed that the strong statistical evidence of a correlation between consumption spending and disposable income meant that disposable income caused consumption spending, not the other way around.

Keynes was not in any way socialist or anti-capitalist. He believed strongly in capitalism. He just believed that during a recession, the government can help the economy recover much better than it could do if left alone. He did not advocate government intervention during normal economic times. Keynes strongly opposed long term deficit spending. Increased government spending, as a stimulus measure during recessionary times, could be financed by short term deficits, but this did not translate into a belief that deficits should be run during non-recessionary times. Keynes' position was otherwise unrelated to today's political debate over "big government". Today's political rhetoric often mischaracterizes the positions of Keynes.

Keynes' viewpoints became the consensus view among economists, and this view prevailed throughout his lifetime. He died in 1946. By the time that Monetarists (led by Milton Friedman) came along in the 1950s to challenge the Keynesian point of view, the debate had changed. It was no longer Keynesian vs. Classical. Government intervention during recessions was advocated by both Keynesians and Monetarists; indeed, by almost all mainstream economists. The debate throughout the 1950s and 1960s was about the relative strength of fiscal and monetary policy. Keynesians believed that fiscal policy was more effective, and monetarists believed that monetary policy was more effective.

164

By the 1970s, the debate between Keynesians and Monetarists had changed again, to basically what the debate is about today. By this time, the debate was no longer about the relative effectiveness of fiscal policy vs. monetary policy; the consensus had been reached that both policies were powerful and effective. Instead, the debate came to be about the wisdom of using such tools during non-recessionary times in order to fine-tune the economy. The Keynesian school of thought became associated with government activism, or using such tools during normal times. Monetarists believe that a slow, steady increase in the money supply, regardless of the current economic situation, was the only activist policy that the government needed. Any other activist policy, according to the Monetarists, would be misguided because it would be less effective and less predictable.

That brings us to the current debate between the Keynesian philosophy and the Monetarist philosophy. The basic difference is already mentioned above, but what follows is a look at some of the details of the differences in points of view:

The Wealth Effect: How much a change in the price level will cause a change in consumer spending, and therefore the ability of the economy to self-correct when it produces at a level of output other than the full-employment level, depends on how steep the aggregate demand curve is. If the aggregate demand curve is steep, then it would take a very large change in the price level to cause the wealth effect to bring the economy back to the full-employment level. If the aggregate demand curve is flat, then a small change in the price level will bring about the self-correcting mechanisms that will put the economy back to full-employment. Keynesians believe that the aggregate demand curve is steep, and therefore activist government policy is needed; the self-correcting mechanism would be inadequate. Monetarists believe that the aggregate demand curve is flat, and that only a modest change in the price level will bring about full-employment due to the wealth effect. This view means that activist policy is not needed.

Money Supply Targets: The Fed (central bank) announces its target for the rate of growth in the money supply each year. Monetarists believe that the money supply is the key factor in influencing economic activity. That is why they advocate modest increases in the money supply as the only activist government policy. With this view, Monetarists believe that the target for the money supply growth should be set low and in a narrow range, and rigorously adhered to. The Keynesian view is different. Keynesians do not believe that such a rigid link exists between the money supply and economic activity. Therefore, they advocate setting the targets in a broad range, so that leeway exists to change as economic conditions change.

Velocity of Money: The velocity of money determines the multiplier effect on real output to a given supply of money. Monetarists believe that the velocity of money is stable, and therefore any changes in the money supply will have a predictable and powerful effect on aggregate spending. In their view, fiscal policy has little effect on the velocity of money and therefore is relatively ineffective. Keynesians also believe that monetary policy is powerful, but they view the velocity of money as being unstable and unpredictable. In this view, the unpredictability of the velocity of money means that fiscal policy is at least as powerful and effective as monetary policy. Note that the view is "at least as powerful", not necessarily "much more powerful". This difference is one of the misconceptions of Keynesian economics.

Inflation: A statistical correlation exists between the level of the money supply and the rate of inflation. When the money supply grows faster, inflation becomes higher. Monetarists view this statistical correlation as one of cause and effect. They believe that a larger money supply always increases inflation. Keynesians do not believe that this cause and effect relationship is necessarily true. The Keynesian viewpoint is aided by the fact that in statistics, a correlation does not imply cause and effect.

An example of inflation will emphasize this difference: Suppose that higher input prices, caused by a supply shock, caused aggregate supply to decrease. This would lower output and employment, but it would also cause the general price level to increase (a leftward shift in the upward-sloping aggregate supply curve). The central bank, in order to move output back to the full-employment level, decides to increase aggregate demand by increasing the money supply, which gives consumers more money to spend. This increase in aggregate demand will increase the equilibrium output level, hopefully to the point of full-employment. But this also will cause a rise in the general price level (a rightward shift in the downward-sloping aggregate demand curve). The overall result is a decrease in aggregate supply, an increase in aggregate demand, output and employment returning to the full employment level, but higher prices. The monetarist view of all of this is that the increase in the money supply is what causes the price level to increase. Keynesians and other critics of the Monetarist position note that other forces caused the central bank to take action. Prices had already begun to rise before the increase in the money supply, and therefore it is not the increase in the money supply that caused the inflation.

Interest Rates: Monetarists believe that interest rates are the key factor in determining savings and investment. They believe that market equilibrium interest rates will bring about a balance between savings and investment. Keynesians note that savings and investments are made by different sets of people. They believe that interest rates are not the key factor in determining savings, but rather disposable income is. In this view, activist policy targeting disposable income is more effective than allowing the market interest rates to set the amount of savings and investment.

About the Author

Jerry Wyant, BSBA Economics University of Missouri

Website: http://www.economicsonlinetutor.com

Economics Facebook page:
http://www.facebook.com/economicsonlinetutor

Education Facebook page:
http://www.facebook.com/MakingEducationWork

Home: Creston, Iowa

Family: wife Linda, daughter Lillie

Sources used:

My own website is the direct source for this entire book:

http://www.economicsonlinetutor.com

In compiling the website, I frequently used the following sources:

Black, Hashimzade and Myles. OXFORD DICTIONARY OF ECONOMICS. Oxford: Oxford University Press, 2009

Boyles, William, and Melvin, Michael. ECONOMICS, 6TH EDITION. Boston: Houghton Mifflin Company, 2005

MERRIAM-WEBSTER'S COLLEGIATE DICTIONARY, 11th Edition. Springfield, MA: Merriam-Webster, Incorporated, 2008

Ragan, James F, Jr and Thomas, Lloyd B, Jr. **PRINCIPLES OF ECONOMICS, 2ND EDITION**. Fort Worth: The Dryden Press, 1993.

Dictionary

What follows is a list of terms and their definitions that are used in the study of economics and that also appear in BASIC ECONOMICS FOR STUDENTS AND NON-STUDENTS ALIKE. Many of these terms have more than one meaning for different contexts, but only one meaning as used here. To avoid confusion caused by multiple definitions, I have used my own wording in order to define each term according to its usage in BASIC ECONOMICS FOR STUDENTS AND NON-STUDENTS ALIKE

The terms are listed in alphabetical order.

<u>Absolute advantage</u>: When one person or country can produce more total output of a commodity than another person or country. This is based on total resources available and is not related to comparative advantage or opportunity costs.

<u>Accounting profit</u>: Profit of a firm that is calculated by subtracting explicit costs from total revenue. This is the amount of profit that shows up on a company's income statement. It differs from economic profit in that economic profit also takes into consideration implicit costs, or opportunity costs.

<u>Activist government policy</u>: Government's use of discretionary fiscal and monetary policies in order to try to create a specific outcome in the economy.

<u>AD</u>: Aggregate demand. Total of all planned expenditures in the economy. This is equal to the sum of consumption spending, gross private domestic investment, government purchases of goods and services, and net exports. In equilibrium, it is equal to real GDP.

<u>AFC</u>: Average fixed cost. Total fixed cost divided by the number of units of output.

<u>Aggregate demand</u>: Total of all planned expenditures in the economy. This is equal to the sum of consumption spending, gross private domestic investment, government purchases of goods and services, and net exports. In equilibrium, it is equal to real GDP.

Aggregate demand and aggregate supply equilibrium: In the aggregate demand & aggregate supply model, the point where the aggregate demand curve and the aggregate supply curve intersect. In equilibrium, no forces exist for changes in the price level or the level of real output (real GDP).

Aggregate demand and aggregate supply model: A diagram showing the aggregate demand curve and the aggregate supply curve, with the price level on the vertical axis and real GDP on the horizontal axis.

Aggregate demand curve: A graph of aggregate demand. This would be a downward sloping curve indicating a negative relationship between planned expenditures and the price level.

Aggregate supply: The amount of real GDP that firms are willing to supply at every price level.

Aggregate supply curve: A graph of aggregate supply. This would be an upward sloping curve indicating a positive relationship between the amount of real output supplied and the price level.

Allocative efficiency: Producing what the consumers want at a price equal to marginal cost.

Anticipated inflation: The inflation rate that is expected to occur in the future. This would be included in the nominal interest rate. Also called expected inflation.

Anti-competitive behavior: Actions by firms that are designed to limit the amount of competition in an industry.

Anti-dumping laws: A restriction on imports of goods that are sold on the world market at unfairly low prices.

Antitrust laws: Laws imposed by governments for the purpose of increasing competition.

APP: Average physical product. Total physical product divided by the number of units of a variable input.

AS: Aggregate supply. The amount of real GDP that firms are willing to supply at every price level.

ATC: Average total cost. Total cost divided by the number of units of output.

Automatic stabilizers: Features of the economy or government policy that offset the effects of the business cycle, without any specific government action taken at the time.

AVC: Average variable cost. Total variable cost divided by the total number of units of output.

Average fixed cost: Total fixed cost divided by the number of units of output.

Average physical product: Total physical product divided by the number of units of a variable input.

Average total cost: Total cost divided by the number of units of output.

Average variable cost: Total variable cost divided by the total number of units of output.

Balance of payments: A record of a country's trade with the rest of the world. This includes all debit and credit transactions in both the current account and the financial account, and must always equal zero (total debits equal total credits).

Balance of trade: The balance in the current account or the merchandise account. A credit balance would be a trade surplus, and a debit balance would be a trade deficit.

Bank: Financial intermediary that accepts deposits and uses deposited funds to make loans.

Bank regulations: Laws that govern the operation of banks.

Bank reserves: Deposits at a bank that have not been loaned out.

Banking system: Collectively, all banks in an economy, including any central bank.

Barometric firm: Price leadership system in oligopoly in which one firm announces a price change, after which other firms in the industry match the price change.

Barriers to entry: Anything that makes it difficult for new firms to enter into a market. This could include high startup (fixed) costs, government regulations, or anti-competitive behavior of existing firms.

Barter economy: An economy in which goods and services are exchanged for other goods and services, without the use of money.

Base year: A year designated, sometimes arbitrarily, as the starting point for comparison of price changes over time. The base year has a price index equal to 100.

Black market: Economic activity that is not reported for tax purposes and is not included in official government statistics. Also called the underground economy, hidden economy, shadow economy, informal economy, and parallel economy.

Boom period: The portion of the business cycle that represents economic expansion, or growth in real GDP.

Bounded rationality: The assumption in economics that the choices people make are done rationally, based on the information known at the time, in an attempt to maximize their satisfaction. This is also known as rational self-interest.

Breakeven price: The price at which total revenue will equal total cost.

Budget: The amount of spending for specific purposes available to individuals, firms, or governments.

Budget constraint: The maximum amount that can be spent due to a limited budget.

Budget line: A graph of a budget constraint.

Bundle of goods: A set of specific goods and quantities used to compare price changes over time.

Business: A private organization that produces goods and / or services. The term as used here is interchangeable with firm, business firm, company, enterprise, and producer.

Business cycle: The idea that economic growth is not constant, but has periods of growth and contraction. The four stages of the business cycle are expansion, peak, contraction, and trough. Macroeconomics is largely concerned with the business cycle.

Business firm: A private organization that produces goods and / or services. The term as used here is interchangeable with firm, company, enterprise, business, and producer.

Business sector: The sector of the economy that offers goods and services for sale. This would include all business firms.

Cap and trade: A policy of using marketable permits as a means of reducing a negative externality.

Capacity: The maximum output of a firm with a given level of fixed inputs.

Capital: In economics, the term capital generally refers to physical capital, or manufactured products such as machinery and equipment that are used in production. This is different from financial capital, which refers to forms of financing.

Capital consumption allowance: The replacement cost of worn-out or damaged machinery and equipment. This mostly consists of depreciation, and the terms are often used interchangeably.

Cartel: An organization of suppliers that agrees formally or informally to restrict competition among themselves in order to maximize the profits of the entire cartel instead of maximizing the profits of individual firms.

Causes of inflation: The causes of inflation are categorized as those that relate to aggregate demand, called demand-pull inflation, and those that relate to aggregate supply, called cost-push inflation.

Centralized decision making: Economic decisions that are made by a central government.

Ceteris paribus: Latin for "other things being equal". A tool of economic analysis that assumes other factors remain constant in order to focus on the relationship between the factors being considered at any point in time.

Chained Consumer Price Index (Chained CPI): An alternative to the CPI index designed to decrease upward bias involving the substitution effect.

Change in demand: A change in a determinant of demand which would change the quantity demanded at every potential price. A change in demand would shift the entire demand curve. The determinants of demand are: consumer income, consumer tastes, the prices of related goods (substitutes and complements), consumer expectations, and the number of potential buyers.

Change in quantity demanded: A change in the quantity of a good or service that consumers would be willing and able to purchase, due to a change in the price of the good or service in question. This would be shown as a movement along an existing demand curve as opposed to a shift in the demand curve.

Change in quantity supplied: A change in the quantity of a good or service that producers are willing and able to offer for sale due to a change in the price of the good or service in question. This would be shown as a movement along an existing supply curve as opposed to a shift in the supply curve.

Change in supply: A change in a determinant of supply which would change the quantity supplied at every potential price. A change in supply would shift the entire supply curve. The determinants of supply are: the prices of resources, technology and productivity, expectations of producers, the number of suppliers, and the prices of alternative goods and services that a firm could produce.

Circular flow model: A model in economics showing the inter-relationships between different sectors of an economy. These inter-relationships include flows of inputs and output; physical products and financial assets; leakages and injections. The sectors of the economy are: households; firms; the government sector; the international sector; and financial intermediaries.

Classical economics: The traditional economic school of thought associated with zero government activist policies. This school of thought involves the assumption that the business cycle and economy are self-correcting.

Coincident indicators: Variables that tend to change at the same time that the business cycle changes stages.

COLA: Cost of Living Adjustment. An automatic adjustment to wages or prices based on the rate of inflation.

Collusion: Cooperation among firms in an oligopoly industry based on secret agreements.

Command economy: An economic system in which economic decisions are made by a central authority.

Communism: A political philosophy in which utopia can be reached through a series of stages in the economy. First, a market economy is replaced by a command economy. Eventually the government sector will disappear, leaving the people to make economic decisions for the common good, without the aid of market forces. Since the last stage only exists in theory, and all governments that are based on the communist philosophy have succeeded in only advancing as far as the command economy, communism is closely associated with socialism.

Company: A private organization that produces goods and / or services. The term as used here is interchangeable with firm, business firm, enterprise, business, and producer.

Comparative advantage: The advantage one person or country has because of a lower opportunity cost in one specific activity, such as production of a specific good.

Complements: Goods that tend to be purchased together, as if they form a unit. A change in the price of one good would cause the demand for a complement to change in the opposite direction.

Consumer: The purchaser of a final good or service. Collectively, consumers comprise the household sector of the economy.

Consumer equilibrium: A situation in which a consumer has maximized utility, at the point where the marginal utility per cost for every consumption choice is equal. Also known as the Equimarginal Principle.

Consumer Price Index: CPI. A measurement of price changes for a "typical" bundle of goods purchased by consumers.

Consumer sector: The sector of the economy that purchases final goods and services.

Consumer surplus: The difference between what consumers are willing to pay and the amount that they actually pay. On a supply and demand diagram, consumer surplus would be the area that lies below the demand curve and above the market price.

Consumption: Overall spending in the economy by the household sector.

Contraction: The portion of the business cycle in which real GDP is falling. This would be associated with a recession and high unemployment.

Cost of living adjustment: An automatic adjustment to wages or prices based on the rate of inflation. Commonly referred to as COLA.

Cost-push inflation: Inflation caused by a decrease in aggregate supply. A decrease in aggregate supply is also associated with an increase in unemployment. The combination of an increase in inflation and an increase in unemployment is called stagflation. If the cause of the decrease in aggregate supply is a sudden increase in the price of a key product or resource in the economy, it is called a supply shock.

CPI: Consumer Price Index. A measurement of price changes for a "typical" bundle of goods purchased by consumers.

Cross elasticity of demand: A measure of the amount that the demand for one good changes due to a change in the price of another good. A cross elasticity of demand that is not equal to zero will indicate that the goods are related. A positive elasticity indicates substitutes. A negative elasticity indicates complements. Same as cross-price elasticity of demand.

Cross-price elasticity of demand: A measure of the amount that the demand for one good changes due to a change in the price of another good. A cross elasticity of demand that is not equal to zero will indicate that the goods are related. A positive elasticity indicates substitutes. A negative elasticity indicates complements. Same as cross elasticity of demand.

Crowding out: A reduction in consumption or investment caused by government deficit spending.

Current account: The combination of the merchandise account, services account, income account, and unilateral transfers account. Associated with net exports and a trade deficit or surplus.

Cyclical unemployment: The portion of unemployment associated with a downturn in the economy, which would be the contraction stage of the business cycle.

Decentralized decision making: Economic activity in which the cumulative effect of decisions of individuals in the economy determine prices and output.

Decrease in demand: A change in demand in which the quantity demanded decreases at every potential price. The demand curve shifts to the left.

Decrease in supply: A change in supply in which the quantity supplied decreases at every potential price. The supply curve shifts to the left.

Debt: The balance of all outstanding government obligations arising from deficit spending.

Deficit: The amount by which government expenditures exceeds tax revenue in a given year.

Deflation: A period of time in which the general price level decreases. Alternatively, a period of time in which the purchasing power of the currency increases.

Demand: The quantities that consumers would be willing and able to purchase at every potential price. When shown on a graph, it becomes a demand curve.

Demand curve: A graph of the demand schedule. The demand curve is a downward sloping curve, indicating a negative relationship between price and quantity demanded.

Demand for money: The quantity of money that people want to hold at each potential interest rate. An inverse relationship exists between the interest rate and the quantity of money demanded.

Demand schedule: A table of demand.

Demand side economics: Discretionary government policies designed to influence the level of aggregate demand in the economy.

Demand-pull inflation: Inflation caused by an increase in aggregate demand.

Deposit expansion multiplier: The maximum amount by which a deposit in a bank can increase the money supply throughout the banking system. It is the reciprocal of the reserve requirement. Also called the money multiplier.

Depreciation: The replacement cost of worn-out machinery and equipment.

Determinants of demand: Factors that determine the quantity demanded at every potential price. Determinants of demand are consumer income, consumer tastes, the prices of complements, the prices of substitutes, consumer expectations, and the number of potential buyers.

Determinants of supply: Factors that determine the quantity supplied at every potential price. Determinants of supply are the prices of resources, technology and productivity, expectations of producers, the number of suppliers, and the prices of alternative goods and services that the firm could produce.

DI: Disposable income. The amount of personal income available for spending or saving after personal income taxes.

Differentiated products: Products of competing firms that consumers consider to be close substitutes, but not identical.

Diminishing marginal returns: The concept that after some output level, output per unit of input will decrease.

Discouraged workers: People without jobs who have given up looking for work, and are no longer active in their job searches. These people are not counted as being part of the total labor force, and are not counted as unemployed. They are not part of the unemployment statistics.

Discount rate: The rate that the Fed charges banks for loans directly from the Fed.

Discretionary fiscal policy: Government fiscal policies designed to achieve specific economic outcomes.

Diseconomies of scale: Production levels above the minimum point on the long run average cost curve.

Disequilibrium: A situation in which equilibrium does not exist. Disequilibrium means that incentives for change exist.

Disposable income: The amount of personal income available for spending or saving after personal income taxes.

Dominant firm: A firm in an oligopoly market that has a much larger market share than any of its competitors.

Earnings: Income received by the factors of production.

Economic approach: The methodology, including the thinking process, or logic, used by economists. Also called economic thinking.

Economic efficiency: A situation in which both productive efficiency and allocative efficiency exist.

Economic good: Something that wouldn't exist in sufficient quantities if it were free.

Economic growth: An increase in real GDP.

Economic indicators: Variables that tend to move along with the business cycle. They include leading indicators, coincident indicators, and lagging indicators.

Economic problem: Scarcity. The fact that resources are finite, but human wants are infinite.

Economic profit: Profit above the level required to keep a firm operating at its current output level. It is profit that is left over after deducting implicit (opportunity) costs. The existence of positive economic profits means that a business is more profitable than alternatives, and in a competitive environment will attract new competition.

Economic schools of thought: Advocacy of different economic policies based on competing economic theories.

Economic system: The method used by a country to control the production, distribution, and consumption of goods and services.

Economic thinking: The methodology, including the thinking process, or logic, used by economists. Also called the economic approach.

Economics: The study of how people choose to use their scarce resources in an attempt to satisfy their unlimited wants. Economics deals with the questions of what to produce, how to produce it, and who to distribute it to.

Economies of scale: A situation where increasing the size of a firm in the long run will decrease unit costs. This occurs on the downward sloping portion of the long run average cost curve.

Economist: A person who specializes in economics.

Economy: All activities involving production, distribution, and consumption within a specified area, such as a geographic area (local, national, global, etc.).

Efficiency: Having the maximum benefit at the lowest cost.

Elasticity: A measure of the responsiveness of one variable to a change in another variable. This measurement is found by dividing the percentage change in one variable by the percentage change in the other variable. The absolute value of the result will necessarily center on the number one: if the result is greater than one, it means that the result is elastic; if the result is less than one, it means that the result is inelastic; and if the result is equal to one, it means that the result is unit elastic. An elasticity value is simply a number with no units attached to it.

Elasticity of demand: A measure of the responsiveness of quantity demanded to a change in price. Also known as the price elasticity of demand.

Elasticity of supply: A measure of the responsiveness of quantity supplied to a change in price.

Embargo: Government trade restriction that forbids the import of a specific good or the import of goods from a specific nation. Also known as a trade embargo.

Enterprise: A private organization that produces goods and / or services. The term as used here is interchangeable with firm, business firm, company, business, and producer.

Entrepreneurship: A resource of production that involves the contribution of organizational skills and / or the supply of financial capital in the hopes of earning a profit.

Equilibrium: A situation in which no incentives for changes exist.

Equimarginal principle: When a consumer has maximized utility, which is the point where the marginal utility per cost for every consumption choice is equal. Also known as consumer equilibrium.

Excess capacity: The ability of a firm to increase production in the short run, without having to change any fixed inputs.

Excess reserves: The amount of reserves held by a bank that is available for loans.

Exchange rate: The ratio of the value of one currency to another, used to conduct transactions involving different currencies.

Excise tax: A tax on the consumption per unit on specific goods. Often called a sin tax.

Expansion: The phase of the business cycle in which real GDP is increasing.

Expectations of consumers: The expectations that consumers have that the price of a good or service will change in the future.

Expectations of producers: The expectations that producers have that the price of a good or service will change in the future.

Expected inflation: The inflation rate that is expected to occur in the future. This rate would be included in the nominal interest rate. Also called anticipated inflation.

Expenditures approach: The method of calculating GDP by adding up all the expenditures in the economy. The formula is GDP=C+I+G+(X-M).

Explicit cost: A cost that involves actual payment being made. This would be every cost except implicit cost, which in economics generally refers to opportunity cost.

Exports: Goods produced domestically but sold to consumers in foreign countries.

External benefit: A benefit received by someone who doesn't pay for it. A positive externality.

External cost: A cost that is not paid for by those imposing the cost or those receiving the benefit. A negative externality.

Externality: A cost or benefit that does not go to those involved in the activity that produces the cost or benefit. A form of market failure.

Factor market: Supply and demand for factors of production.

Factors of demand: The price of the good in question, plus other things that determine the level of demand, called determinants of demand: consumer income, consumer tastes, the prices of complements, the prices of substitutes, consumer expectations, and the number of potential buyers. The price of the good in question is plotted on the supply and demand diagram, so any change in price would involve a movement along the demand curve. The determinants of demand are not plotted on the supply and demand diagram, so any changes in any of them would involve the demand curve being shifted.

Factors of production: Resources used in the production of goods and services: land, labor, and capital. Some economists classify entrepreneurship as a fourth factor of production while other economists classify entrepreneurship as a special class of labor.

Factors of supply: The price of the good in question, plus other things that determine the level of supply, called determinants of supply: the prices of resources, technology and productivity, expectations of producers, the number of suppliers, and the prices of alternative goods and services that the firm can produce (opportunity costs). The price of the good in question is plotted on the supply and demand diagram, so any change in price would involve a movement along the supply curve. The determinants of supply are not plotted on the supply and demand diagram, so any changes in any of them would involve the supply curve being shifted.

Fallacy of composition: The fallacy of logic that involves saying that what applies to one will also apply to many.

FED: The Federal Reserve System. The central bank of the United States.

Federal funds rate: The interest rate charged for overnight borrowing between banks in the United States.

Federal Reserve System: The central bank of the United States.

Fiat money: Currency that is not backed by any commodities, but rather is only backed by the faith and credit of the issuing government. Also called fiduciary money.

Fiduciary money: Currency that is not backed by any commodities, but rather is only backed by the faith and credit of the issuing government. Also called fiat money.

Final goods and services: Goods and services available to the ultimate consumer.

Financial account: The balance of payments account representing the flow of money between nations.

Financial capital: Financial backing in the form of personal savings, stocks, bonds, bank loans, etc., used for the costs of a business.

Financial intermediary: An organization, such as a bank, that accepts deposits and makes loans.

Firm: A private organization that produces goods and/or services. The term as used here is interchangeable with business firm, company, enterprise, business, and producer.

Fiscal policy: Government policy regarding government spending and taxing decisions. Often discussed in terms of discretionary fiscal policy, or policy designed to produce a specific economic outcome.

Fixed cost: A cost that does not change with the level of output. Fixed costs only exist in the short run, the time frame in which one or more of the factors of production cannot be changed.

Fixed income: Personal income that is set at a specified amount, and can only be changed if it is indexed for inflation. Includes such income types as pension payments and Social Security payments.

Flow concept: A flow is something that is measured over a period of time rather than at one specific point in time, which would be a stock concept. For example, standard accounting statements include an income statement, which is a flow concept, and a balance sheet, which is a stock concept.

Foreign exchange: Economic activity between people in different countries.

Foreign exchange market: A global market in which people trade one currency for another.

Fractional reserve system: A system in banking in which banks are allowed to loan out an amount equal to a fraction of its reserves.

Free good: Something that there would be enough of if it was free. A good that is not scarce.

Free market: A market where transactions occur voluntarily, without government interference.

Frictional unemployment: Unemployment caused by a time lag between the time a person begins searching for a job and the time that the person is hired for a job.

Friedman, Milton: Economist who is considered to be the father of the monetarist economic school of thought.

Full employment: Old term, still used in some economics textbooks, for the natural rate of unemployment.

Functions of money: What characterizes a money economy as opposed to a barter economy: medium of exchange, unit of account, and store of value.

Game theory: A branch of mathematics often used in economics to explain strategic behavior.

GDP: Gross domestic product. The market value of all final goods and services produced in a year within a country's borders.

GDP deflator: A price index used in the calculations for real GDP. Also known as a GDP price index.

GDP gap: The amount by which actual GDP is below potential GDP. Also known as a GDP output gap or an output gap.

GDP output gap: The amount by which actual GDP is below potential GDP. Also known as a GDP gap or an output gap.

GDP price index: A price index used in the calculation for real GDP. Also known as a GDP deflator.

GDPPI: GDP price index. A price index used in the calculation for real GDP.

Global economy: The concept that economies around the world are increasingly interdependent; Globalization.

Globalization: The concept that economies around the world are increasingly interdependent; Global economy.

GNP: Gross National Product. The total value of all goods and services produced by a nation's citizens, regardless of which nation the production takes place in.

Gold standard: An economy in which the value of the currency is tied to the value of gold. The currency can be exchanged for an equal value of gold upon demand.

Goods: Something that people prefer to have more of than less.

Goods and services: A term used in economics meaning the output of firms. Often the term goods is used interchangeably with goods and services in order to avoid repetition in a discussion.

Government intervention: Any government involvement in economic activity.

Government bonds: A method that governments use to finance expenditures. The government issues bonds to the public in order to finance deficit spending. Outstanding bonds represent the government's debt.

Government purchases: Government spending for the purchase of goods and services. Not all government spending is included: transfer payments are excluded.

Government sector: The role that the government plays in the economic activity of a country.

Government transfer payments: Payments made by governments to one group of people, financed by taxing a different group of people.

Great Depression: The deep worldwide economic downturn that lasted from the late 1920s through much of the 1930s. The Great Depression could not be explained by classical economic theory, so new economic schools of thought were developed, starting with Keynesian Economics.

Gross domestic product: The market value of all final goods and services produced in a year within a country's borders.

Gross investment: Total spending by businesses on the factors of production. The difference between gross investment and net investment is depreciation. Gross investment is considered to be interest-sensitive. Also called gross private domestic investment.

Gross national product: The total value of all goods and services produced by a nation's citizens, regardless of which nation the production takes place in.

Gross private domestic investment: Total spending by businesses on the factors of production. The difference between gross investment and net investment is depreciation. Gross investment is considered to be interest-sensitive. Also called gross investment.

Hidden economy: Economic activity that is not reported for tax purposes and is not included in official government statistics. Also known as the black market, underground economy, shadow economy, informal economy, and parallel economy.

Hidden employed: Workers in the underground economy. This employment does not show up in the official employment statistics.

Hidden unemployed: Discouraged workers and underemployed workers. They are not counted as unemployed in the unemployment statistics.

Homogeneous products: Products of different firms that have no differences in the minds of consumers. Consumers do not prefer the products of one firm over another. The products are considered to be perfect substitutes. Also known as identical products and standardized products.

Household sector: The sector of the economy that represents the final consumers of goods and services, and also provides the factors of production to the business sector.

Hyperinflation: A situation in which the rate of inflation accelerates to the point where the entire economy breaks down.

Identical products: Products of different firms that have no differences in the minds of consumers. Consumers do not prefer the products of one firm over the products of another firm. The products are considered to be perfect substitutes. Also known as homogeneous products and standardized products.

Implicit costs: Costs for which no actual payment takes place. In economics, implicit costs generally refer to opportunity costs.

Import quota: A trade restriction in which the government limits the amount of a good, or the amount of goods from a specific country that can be imported.

Imports: Transactions in which the products purchased have been produced in another country.

Increase in demand: A change in a determinant of demand which causes the quantity demanded to increase at every potential price. This is represented on a supply and demand diagram as a rightward shift in the demand curve.

Increase in supply: A change in a determinant of supply which causes the quantity supplied to increase at every potential price. This is represented on a supply and demand diagram as a rightward shift in the supply curve.

Increasing opportunity costs: The concept that as more and more resources are devoted to a particular activity, the marginal cost becomes increasingly higher. This concept explains the bowed-out (convex) shape of the PPC.

Income: Payments received (earnings) by the factors of production.

Income account: The portion of the current account in the balance of payments that includes transactions involving income between countries. Investment income and wages earned in another country is a positive (credit). Investment income and wages earned from domestic activity by foreigners is a negative (debit).

Income approach: A method of calculating GDP by adding up the income received by the factors of production. The formula is: GDP = compensation of employees + net interest + rent + profits (proprietors' income + corporate profits) + indirect business taxes + capital consumption allowance (or depreciation) - net factor income from abroad.

Income elasticity of demand: A measurement of the responsiveness of quantity demanded to a change in income.

Indicators: Variables that tend to change as the phase of the business cycle changes. Also known as economic indicators. Indicators can be leading indicators, coincident indicators, or lagging indicators.

Indifference curve: A graph plotting all combinations of the quantities of two goods for which a consumer has no preference.

Indifference analysis: A simplified, graphical economic model that helps to explain consumer choices.

Indifference map: A graph showing various indifference curves as well as a budget line.

Indirect business taxes: Taxes collected through businesses that are not related to the amount of income. Indirect business taxes include sales taxes and excise taxes.

Industry: A sector of the economy in which firms use similar resources to produce similar products. In economics, industry is often used interchangeably with market.

Inelastic: A variable that is relatively unresponsive to changes in another variable. Elasticity with an absolute value of less than one.

Infant industry: An industry that currently cannot compete with more efficient foreign competition, but is believed to be capable of becoming competitive if the government imposes trade restrictions to protect the industry while it grows.

Inferior good: A good for which demand changes in the opposite direction as income.

Inflation: A sustained rise in the average level of prices. Alternatively, a sustained decline in the purchasing power of the currency.

Inflation rate: The percentage change in the average price level from one year to the next.

Informal economy: Economic activity that is not reported for tax purposes and is not included in official government statistics. Also known as the black market, underground economy, hidden economy, shadow economy, and parallel economy.

Infrastructure: Basic public institutions and facilities including an education system and a system of roads and bridges.

Inputs: The use of factors of production. Used interchangeably with the term resources.

Interest: Payment made for the use of somebody else's money.

Interest rate: The amount of interest, as an annualized percentage of the principle amount of a loan.

Interest rate effect: A price factor of aggregate demand. As the price level increases, more money is needed for purchases. This increases the transaction demand for money, and lowers the demand for other financial assets such as bonds. A lower demand for bonds will decrease the price of bonds, increasing interest rates. Higher interest rates will create a decrease in aggregate investment spending.

Intermediate goods: Goods that are produced for use in producing other goods.

Intermediate target: A goal for which another goal is the real aim. For example, the Fed uses a target level of the money supply in order to achieve another goal, which is a desired level of real output and prices.

International cartel: A cartel composed of firms from different countries.

International sector: The sector of the economy that involves other countries. This would be the import and export components of the economy.

International trade effect: A price factor of aggregate demand. Changes in the relative prices of foreign and domestic goods will cause changes in net exports. These changes will change the overall price level, creating a movement along the aggregate demand curve.

Intersection: On a graph, the point where two curves cross, usually indicating a point of equilibrium.

Inventory: Goods that have been produced but not yet sold.

Investment: In economics, investment generally refers to physical investment, which is spending by firms, or the business sector of the economy; as opposed to financial investment, which refers to spending by people on financial assets for the purpose of earning a profit.

Key resource: A scarce resource for which there are no close substitutes.

Keynes, John Maynard: Economist who developed Keynesian Economics, which challenged classical economic thinking during the Great Depression by advocating for targeted government activism.

Keynesian Economics: The economic school of thought that developed as a result of the theories of John Maynard Keynes. This school of thought has evolved over time and is no longer identical to the actual theories of Keynes.

Kinked demand curve: In oligopoly theory, a demand curve composed of different segments of two demand curves with different elasticity and slopes, thus forming a kink at the point where the two curves are joined.

Labor: The input that involves the physical and intellectual services of people, including training, education, and peoples' abilities.

Labor force: The number of employed persons plus the number of persons counted as unemployed. Also known as the total labor force.

Labor force participation rate: The percentage of the working age population that is counted in the total labor force.

Labor market: The supply and demand for workers.

Lagging indicators: Variables that tend to change after a change in the phase of the business cycle.

Laissez-faire: The economic concept that efficiency in the economy is best achieved through government non-intervention, so that people are left alone to pursue their own self interests.

Land: The factor of production that includes minerals, timber, and water, as well as the actual land itself.

Law of demand: "The quantity of a specific good or service that people are willing and able to purchase decreases as the price increases, and increases as the price decreases, as long as the price is the only thing that changes."

Law of supply: "The quantity of a specific good or service that producers are willing and able to offer for sale increases as the price increases, and decreases as the price decreases, as long as the price is the only thing that changes."

Leading indicators: Variables that tend to change prior to a change in the phase of the business cycle.

Limited resources: The part of the scarcity concept of economics that says that resources are not infinite.

Liquidity trap: A theory that a certain nominal interest rate exists where expansionary monetary policy would be ineffective in lowering interest rates any further.

Long run: A time frame long enough to make all inputs variable. No fixed inputs or fixed costs exist in the long run. Also called the planning horizon.

Long run aggregate supply curve: With the theory that in the long run all costs and prices have time to adjust, higher prices will not increase profits and therefore will not lead to an increase in real GDP. This makes the long run aggregate supply curve a vertical line. Many economists believe that the level of output associated with the vertical long run aggregate supply curve is at the level of potential GDP (the natural rate of unemployment).

Long run average total cost: In the long run, all costs are variable, and all short run situations are possible. The long run average total cost curve connects all possible short run average total cost curves. This can take different shapes, but a downward sloping portion would indicate economies of scale while an upward sloping portion would indicate diseconomies of scale.

Long run Phillips Curve: Many economists believe that in the long run the actual unemployment rate will equal the natural rate of unemployment. In this case, the long run Phillips Curve is a vertical line at the natural rate of unemployment. This would indicate that no trade-off exists between inflation and unemployment in the long run.

Lowest cost firm: A form of price leadership in oligopoly in which the firm with the lowest costs is the price leader.

LRATC: Long run average total cost. In the long run, all costs are variable, and all short run situations are possible. The long run average total cost curve connects all possible short run average total cost curves. This can take different shapes, but a downward sloping portion would indicate economies of scale while an upward sloping portion would indicate diseconomies of scale.

Luxury good: A good with a high income elasticity of demand.

Macroeconomics: The study of economics at the level of the economy as a whole, or an entire industry or sector of the economy as a whole.

Marginal benefit: Additional benefit received as a result of the last choice made.

Marginal cost: The addition to total cost associated with the last unit of output.

Marginal physical product: The addition to total physical product when one more unit of a variable input is added.

Marginal propensity to consume: MPC. The percentage of additional disposable income spent instead of saved.

Marginal propensity to import: MPI. The percentage of additional disposable income spent on imported goods.

Marginal propensity to save: MPS. The percentage of additional disposable income saved instead of spent.

Marginal revenue: MR. The addition to total revenue resulting from one more unit of output sold.

Marginal revenue product: MRP. The addition to total revenue resulting from one more unit of a variable input.

Marginal utility: The addition to total utility resulting from consuming one more unit of a specific good.

Market: A sector of the economy in which firms use similar resources to produce similar products. Often used interchangeably with the term industry.

Market demand curve: The demand curve for an entire market, as opposed to the demand curve for an individual firm or consumer. Equal to the sum of all individual demand curves.

Market economy: An economic system in which market forces are free to determine economic outcomes.

Market failure: A situation in which the free market does not allocate resources to their most efficient uses.

Market power: The ability of one firm to influence market prices.

Market share: The percentage of a market controlled by a specific firm.

Market structure: Refers to a classification economists use to describe firms with similar behavioral characteristics, based on the number of firms in an industry, the similarity of products, ease of entry into the market, and market power.

Market supply curve: The supply curve in an entire market, as opposed to the supply curve for one firm. Equal to the sum of all individual firms' supply curves.

Marketable permits: Permits issued by the government to control the amount of negative externalities.

MC: Marginal cost. The addition to total cost associated with the last unit of output.

Medium of exchange: The function of money meaning that money serves as a means of payment.

Merchandise account: The part of the current account in the balance of payments that refers to the movement of merchandise between nations. Represents exports and imports.

Microeconomics: The study of economics on the individual level: The individual firm, the individual consumer, or the individual worker.

Midpoint formula: A method for calculating elasticity that eliminates the discrepancy created by naming one starting point as opposed to another starting point in the calculation.

Minimum efficient scale: The lowest point on the long run average total cost curve.

Minimum wage laws: Laws that set a price floor for wages.

Mixed economy: An economic system that has features of both a market economy and a command economy.

Model: An approach used in the study of economics that simplifies reality in order to focus attention on a specific relationship between variables.

Monetarists: Economic school of thought developed in the 1940s to oppose the theories of Keynesian Economics.

Monetary policy: Economic policy of the government or central bank relating to the money supply and interest rates.

Monetary policy tools: Tools used by the government or central bank in implementing monetary policy.

Money: Anything that is widely accepted as payment in exchange for goods and services. This definition can be somewhat arbitrary in real world situations, so economists have separated the definition into four different definitions: M-1, M-2, M-3, and L. Money is also defined by its functions: medium of exchange, unit of account, and store of value.

Money demand: In macroeconomics, the amount of money that people want to hold instead of investing in financial instruments. Divided into the transaction demand for money, the precautionary demand for money, and the speculative demand for money.

Money supply: The total amount of money in the economy. The money supply can be controlled by the government or central bank through monetary policy. Since this means the money supply is not based on market forces, the money supply curve is a vertical line.

Money supply targets: Intermediate goal of monetary policy aimed at a specific level of money in the economy.

Monopolistic competition: A market structure characterized by having many competing firms, each small compared to the overall size of the market, selling differentiated products, with easy entry into the market.

Money multiplier: Another name for the deposit expansion multiplier in banking. The maximum amount by which a single deposit in a bank can increase the money supply throughout the banking system. It is the reciprocal of the reserve requirement.

Monopolist: A firm in a monopoly market structure.

Monopoly: A market structure in which one firm supplies the entire market.

MPC: Marginal propensity to consume. The percentage of additional disposable income spent instead of saved.

MPI: Marginal propensity to import. The percentage of additional disposable income spent on imported goods.

MPP: Marginal physical product. The addition to total physical product that results from the addition of one more unit of a variable input.

MPS: Marginal propensity to save. The percentage of additional disposable income saved instead of spent.

MR: Marginal revenue. The addition to total revenue resulting from one more unit of output sold.

MR=MC: Marginal revenue equals marginal cost. The profit maximizing output level for all firms regardless of market structure. Only in perfect competition will this also be the profit maximizing price.

MRP: Marginal revenue product. The addition to total revenue resulting from the addition of one more unit of a variable input.

Multiplier effect: The idea that a change can have an overall effect larger than the initial change. For example, an increase in discretionary government spending can create income for others to spend, resulting in an increase in real GDP larger than the amount of the increase in government spending.

NAIRU: Non-accelerating inflation rate of unemployment. Also known as the natural rate of unemployment. The lowest unemployment rate consistent with not putting upward pressure on prices and wages.

National debt: Total balance of outstanding government obligations, usually from government bonds issued to the public.

National income: Total income received by the factors of production. Employee compensation plus net interest plus rent plus proprietors' income plus corporate profits.

National income accounting: A system of measurements allowing for comparison of the sizes of different economies, as well as measurements of one economy's performance over time.

Natural barriers to entry: A reason for a monopoly to exist: one firm can supply the entire market demand more efficiently that two or more competing firms can. Economies of scale.

Natural monopoly: A monopoly created by natural barriers to entry.

Natural rate of unemployment: The lowest unemployment rate consistent with not putting upward pressure on prices and wages.

NDP: Net domestic product. Gross domestic product minus depreciation.

Necessity: A normal good with a low income elasticity of demand.

Negative correlation: A relationship between variables such that when one variable increases, the other variable decreases.

Negative externalities: Costs accruing to people who are not parties to private transactions.

Net benefit: Excess of benefits over costs.

Net creditor nation: A nation that loans more to all other nations than it borrows. A nation that exports more than it imports.

Net debtor nation: A nation that borrows more from all other nations than it loans. A nation that imports more than it exports.

Net domestic product: NDP. Gross domestic product minus depreciation.

Net exports: Total exports minus total imports. The international sector of an economy.

Net factor income from abroad: Income received by citizens outside the nation's borders minus income received by foreigners within the nation's borders. Also known as net foreign factor income.

Net foreign factor income: Income received by citizens outside the nation's borders minus income received by foreigners within the nation's borders. Also known as net factor income from abroad.

Net investment: Gross private domestic investment minus capital consumption allowance (or depreciation).

Net national product: NNP. National income plus indirect business taxes.

NI: National income. Total income received by the factors of production: Employee compensation plus net interest plus rent plus proprietors' income plus corporate profits.

NNP: Net national product. National income plus indirect business taxes.

Nominal GDP: Total value of GDP measured in current prices.

Nominal interest rate: Actual stated interest rate, equal to the real interest rate plus the anticipated inflation rate.

Nominal value: Value in current prices.

Non-accelerating inflation rate of unemployment: NAIRU. Also known as the natural rate of unemployment. The lowest unemployment rate consistent with not putting upward pressure on prices and wages.

Normal good: A good with a positive income elasticity of demand. A good that people buy more of as income rises.

Normal profits: Profits sufficient to cover opportunity costs and not provide an incentive to change output levels, or cause entry or exit in an industry.

Normative statement: A statement of opinion, not facts; statements that include value judgments. Stating "what ought to be". The opposite of a positive statement.

Oligopoly: A market structure characterized by few firms, each relatively large compared to the overall market size, with relatively difficult entry into the market and at least some control over the prices it sells its product for.

Open market operations: Monetary policy involving the sales and purchases of government bonds.

Opportunity cost: The value of the next best (forgone) choice.

Optimal bundle: In demand analysis, the point on the budget line that touches the outermost indifference curve, indicating a maximum benefit to the consumer.

Output gap: The amount by which actual GDP is below potential GDP. Also known as a GDP gap or a GDP output gap.

Overnight funds: Money borrowed by a bank from another bank, or the central bank, to cover an unexpected shortage of reserves.

Paradox of Saving: Another name for Paradox of Thrift.

Paradox of Thrift: A theory stating that during a recession, a planned increase in savings can cause actual savings to decrease. Also known as Paradox of Saving.

Parallel economy: Economic activity that is not reported for tax purposes and is not included in official government statistics. Also known as the black market, underground economy, hidden economy, shadow economy, and informal economy.

Patent laws: Laws granting monopoly power to creators of new products or processes for a period of time, currently 17 years in the United States.

Peak: The point in the business cycle where expansion ends, and the level of real GDP is maximized for that business cycle.

Per capita: A value divided by the total population, to calculate an average per person.

Perfect competition: A market structure characterized by many firms, each too small to influence the market price, producing identical products, with ease of entry into the market. Considered to be the most efficient market structure, although real life examples are difficult to find.

Perfect substitutes: Products of different firms for which no differences exist in the view of consumers. Identical products.

Perfectly elastic: An elasticity value equal to infinity.

Perfectly inelastic: An elasticity value equal to zero.

Personal income: PI. National income minus income earned but not received plus income received but not earned.

Phillips Curve: A downward sloping curve indicating a trade-off between inflation and unemployment.

Physical capital: Manufactured products such as machinery and equipment that are used in the production of other products. Also known in economics simply as capital.

PI: Personal income. National income minus income earned but not received plus income received but not earned.

Planning horizon: Another name for the long run.

Positive correlation: A relationship between variables such that both variables change in the same direction.

Positive externalities: Benefits accruing to people who are not parties to private transactions.

Positive statement: A statement of facts, without including opinions or value judgments. The opposite of a normative statement.

PPC: Production possibilities curve. An economic model that shows graphically the various combinations of two goods that can be produced using a given level of resources.

PPI: Producer Price Index. A measurement of changes in the prices received by producers. A leading economic indicator for inflation. Formerly known as the Wholesale Price Index.

Precautionary demand for money: The amount of money that the public prefers to hold for spending in emergency situations.

Price ceiling: A price control that sets a maximum price that is allowed to be charged. A common example would be rent control.

Price controls: Government restrictions on the prices that can be charged on specific goods and services.

Price discrimination: The practice of charging different prices to different groups of consumers based on different demand elasticity.

Price elasticity of demand: A measurement of the responsiveness of quantity demanded to a change in price. Also known as elasticity of demand.

Price floor: A price control that sets a minimum price that is allowed to be charged. A common example would be a minimum wage.

Price index: A number assigned to represent the average price level at a specific point in time in order to measure the rate of inflation.

Price leadership: A method for firms in oligopoly to cooperate with one another. One firm, called a price leader, changes its price and other firms follow suit.

Price maker: A firm with significant market power to set its own price.

Price taker: A firm with no market power; it has to accept the price that is established by the market.

Private benefit: A benefit received by a party to a transaction.

Private cost: A cost paid by a party to a transaction.

Private sector: The portion of the economy that does not include the government.

Prisoner's Dilemma: Game theory model used to explain the behavior of firms in oligopoly.

Producer: A private organization that produces goods and / or services. The term as used here is interchangeable with firm, business firm, company, enterprise, and business.

Producer Price Index: PPI. A measurement of changes in the prices received by producers. A leading economic indicator for inflation. Formerly known as the Wholesale Price Index.

Producer surplus: The difference between the price the sellers are willing to sell the product for and the price that the sellers actually receive.

Producer's tax: A tax levied on sellers.

Production bottlenecks: The inability of firms to increase output in the short run due to a lack of excess capacity.

Production Possibilities Curve: PPC. An economic model that shows graphically the various combinations of two goods that can be produced using a given level of resources.

Productive efficiency: Using the least cost combination of resources to produce a specific level of output.

Productivity: The amount of output per unit of input.

Profit: The excess of total revenue over total cost.

Prohibitive barriers to entry: Barriers to entry in an industry high enough to effectively prevent any entry.

Public sector: The portion of the economy represented by the government.

Quantity demanded: The amount of a specific good or service that people are willing and able to purchase at one specific price.

Quantity supplied: The amount of a specific good or service that producers are willing and able to offer for sale at one specific price.

Rate of inflation: The percentage change in the average level of prices from one year to the next.

Rational self-interest: The assumption in economics that the choices people make are done rationally, based on the information known at the time, in an attempt to maximize their satisfaction. Also known as bounded rationality.

Real GDP: Total output of an economy measured in constant prices.

Real GDP per capita: Total output of an economy measured in constant prices, divided by total population.

Real interest rate: The nominal (stated) interest rate minus the anticipated rate of inflation.

Real value: A value that has been adjusted for changes in the average level of prices.

Recession: A period of significant decline in total output, income, employment, and trade, usually lasting from six months to a year, and marked by widespread contractions in many sectors of the economy.

Recessionary gap: A situation in which a GDP gap exists, or when equilibrium real GDP is below potential real GDP.

Redistribution of wealth: Anything that changes the wealth distribution between different groups of people.

Rent: The earnings of land, with land being a factor of production.

Required reserve ratio: The percentage of deposits that banks have to keep on hand, and not make available for loans.

Required reserves: The amount of deposits that a bank has that cannot be loaned out, in order to meet the required reserve ratio.

Reserve ratio: The percentage of deposits at a bank that have not been loaned out.

Reserve requirement: The required reserve ratio.

Reserves: In banking, the deposits at a bank that have not been loaned out. Same as bank reserves.

Resource prices: The prices that producers pay for the use of resources.

Resources: The use of factors of production. Used interchangeably with the term "inputs".

Responsiveness: The amount that one variable will change in response to a change in another variable.

Revenue: Proceeds from sales. Same as total revenue. Equal to price times quantity.

Ricardian Equivalence: The theory that consumers reduce current consumption because of the future tax increases that they believe will occur to pay for the government debt.

Scarcity: Something that is not available in sufficient quantities to satisfy every human want, regardless of price.

Seasonal unemployment: Unemployment that is caused by the slow season in an industry.

Sector: Classification of different portions of the economy: the household sector, the business sector, the government sector, the international sector.

Services: The output of a firm that is not comprised of physical merchandise.

Services account: The portion of the current account of the balance of payments that includes transactions between countries involving services, such as tourism and transportation.

Shadow economy: Economic activity that is not reported for tax purposes and is not included in official government statistics. Also known as the black market, underground economy, hidden economy, informal economy, and parallel economy.

Short run: A time frame sufficiently short enough so that at least one input is fixed.

Short run aggregate supply curve: SRASC. The aggregate supply curve in the short run. It would be upward sloping.

Short run average total cost: The sum of average variable cost and average fixed cost in the short run.

Shortage: The amount by which demand exceeds supply.

Shut down price: The price below which a profit-maximizing firm will shut down in the short run.

Shut down rule: A competitive firm should shut down in the short run if it cannot find an output level that will allow it to cover total variable costs. Otherwise, it should continue to produce.

Silver standard: An economy in which the value of the currency is tied to the value of silver. The currency can be exchanged for an equal value of silver upon demand.

Social benefit: Total benefit of a transaction. Private benefit plus external benefit.

Social cost: Total cost of a transaction. Private cost plus external cost.

Socialism: An economic system in which the government owns the means of production.

Specialization and trade: The concept that individuals or nations should specialize in the production of things for which they have comparative advantage, and trade for the things that they do not have comparative advantage.

Speculative demand for money: The amount of money that the public prefers to hold as a hedge against price changes in other financial assets.

Spending multiplier: The amount by which an increase in spending will increase real GDP. Equal to the reciprocal of leakages: (1 / (MPS + MPI)).

Spillover: The effect that actions of producers or consumers have on people who are not parties to private transactions.

SRATC: Short run average total cost. The sum of average variable cost and average fixed cost in the short run.

Stagflation: A situation in which inflation and unemployment are both rising at the same time.

Standardized products: Products of different firms that have no differences in the minds of consumers. Consumers do not prefer the products of one firm over another firm. The products are considered to be perfect substitutes. Also known as identical products and homogeneous products.

Stock concept: A stock is something that is measured at a specific point in time rather than over a period of time, which would be a flow concept. For example, standard accounting statements include an income statement, which is a flow concept, and a balance sheet, which is a stock concept.

Store of value: The function of money that allows people to make purchases at times that do not coincide with the time that income is received.

Strategic behavior: Actions taken by one that depend on actions taken by another.

Structural unemployment: The type of unemployment caused by a difference between the job skills required to fill the openings available, and the job skills that applicants possess.

Subsidy: A payment made by the government to a domestic producer, effectively decreasing the production costs for domestic production.

Substitutes: Goods consumers consider to be similar enough so that if the price of one increases, consumers will purchase more of another good instead of the one with the price increase.

Supply: The quantities that producers are willing and able to offer for sale at every potential price. When shown on a graph, it becomes a supply curve.

Supply and demand: An economic model that explains market price and quantity outcomes.

Supply and demand equilibrium: The price where the quantity supplied is equal to the quantity demanded. In equilibrium, no market forces for changes exist.

Supply curve: A graph of the supply schedule. The supply curve is an upward sloping curve, indicating a positive relationship between price and quantity supplied.

Supply of money: The quantity of money in the economy. Since the money supply is controlled by the government or the central bank, it is not determined by market forces, and therefore does not change as the price level changes. The money supply curve is a vertical line.

Supply schedule: A table of supply.

Supply shock: Inflation caused by a sudden increase in the price of a key product or resource in the economy.

Supply side economics: Discretionary government policies designed to influence the level of aggregate supply in the economy.

Surplus: In supply and demand analysis, the amount by which supply exceeds demand. In market structure analysis, the benefit received when the market price is different from the price that consumers are willing to pay (consumer surplus), or the price that producers are willing to sell for (producer surplus).

Tariff: A tax on goods imported from another country.

Tax incidence: The degree to which a consumer pays a tax on the sale of a good, and the degree to which the seller pays the tax, based on the price elasticity of demand and supply.

Technology: The processes and knowledge that go into production.

TC: Total cost. The sum of total variable cost and total fixed cost.

TFC: Total fixed cost. The total cost associated with fixed inputs.

Total cost: The sum of total variable cost and total fixed cost.

Total fixed cost: TFC. The total cost associated with fixed inputs.

Total labor force: The number of employed persons plus the number of persons counted as unemployed. Also known simply as the labor force.

Total physical product: The total number of units of output for a given quantity of a variable input. Same as total product.

Total population: The total number of persons living within a nation's borders.

Total product: The total number of units of output for a given quantity of a variable input. Same as total physical product.

Total revenue: TR. Proceeds from sales. Equal to price times quantity.

Total revenue maximization: Total revenue is maximized at the quantity where the demand curve is unit elastic.

Total surplus: The sum of consumer surplus and producer surplus.

Total variable cost: TVC. The variable costs associated with a given level of output. Equal to quantity times average variable cost.

TPP: Total physical product. The total number of units of output for a given quantity of a variable input. Same as total product.

TR: Total revenue. Proceeds from sales. Equal to price times quantity.

Trade deficit: The amount by which imports exceeds exports.

Trade embargo: A trade restriction in which the imports of a specific good, or imports from a specific country, are forbidden.

Trade restrictions: Anything that limits free trade between nations.

Trade subsidy: A payment made by the government to a domestic producer, effectively decreasing the production costs for domestic production.

Trade surplus: The amount by which exports exceeds imports.

Transaction demand for money: The amount of money that the public prefers to hold in order to pay for transactions.

Transfer payments: Money that the government collects from one group of people in the form of taxes, and pays to another group of people in the form of benefits. This portion of government spending does not represent new production in the economy, and therefore is not included in GDP.

Trough: The point in the business cycle when the contraction stage ends.

TVC: Total variable cost. The variable costs associated with a given level of output. Equal to quantity times average variable cost.

Types of unemployment: Unemployment is classified into four categories: cyclical, frictional, structural, and seasonal.

Underemployment: People who are employed but not fully utilizing their abilities. Often refers to part time workers who would prefer to be working full time.

Underground economy: Economic activity that is not reported for tax purposes and is not included in official government statistics. Also known as the black market, hidden economy, shadow economy, informal economy, and parallel economy.

Unemployed persons: People without jobs who are actively searching for work.

Unemployment: Wanting a job, and actively looking for a job, but not having a job.

Unemployment rate: The percentage of the labor force that is classified as unemployed.

Unemployment statistics: Various statistics relating to the labor market, especially the unemployment rate.

Unilateral transfers account: The portion of the current account in the balance of payments that represents transactions between countries in which only one country actually receives something.

Unit elastic: An elasticity in which a change in one variable will result in an equal change in another variable. The elasticity value is equal to one.

Unit of account: The function of money in which the values of different items can be compared based on their prices as measured by the currency.

Unlimited wants: The concept that somebody will always want more of something.

Upward bias: The idea that the official inflation rate is probably higher than the actual inflation rate, due to problems with measurements. One source of upward bias is holding the bundle of goods used in the measurements constant even after the relative prices of the goods involved change. Another source of upward bias is that the price changes are not adjusted for improvements in the quality of the goods over time.

US Treasury Bills: Short term securities issued by the United States government to finance deficit spending. Treasury Bills have a maturity of less than one year from the issue date. They are sold at a discount from par value, and instead of paying a stated interest they simply pay the full par value at maturity. The effective interest rate is determined by the amount of discount in the purchase price.

US Treasury Bonds: Bonds issued by the United States government to finance deficit spending. The maturity date is generally 20 to 30 years from the issue date. Treasury Bonds pay semi-annual interest based on a stated percentage of par value.

US Treasury Notes: Bonds issued by the United States government to finance deficit spending. The maturity date is generally 1 to 10 years from the issue date. Treasury Notes pay semi-annual interest based on a stated percentage of par value.

Utility: A measure of the satisfaction, or happiness, that something gives to an individual.

Variable cost: VC. The cost associated with a factor of production that changes as the level of output changes.

Velocity of money: The average number of times that a given money supply is spent in an economy in one year.

Wages: The price paid to labor.

Wealth effect: A price factor of aggregate demand. With any given amount of financial assets (money, stocks, and bonds), the higher the price level, the lower the purchasing power, and therefore the lower the real wealth.

Wholesale Price Index: Former name for the Producer Price Index.

WPI: Wholesale Price Index. Former name for the Producer Price Index.

CPSIA information can be obtained
at www.ICGtesting.com
Printed in the USA
LVHW051628040221
678389LV00014B/1650